ISRAEL'S
ANGEL
EXTRAORDINARY

ISRAEL'S ANGEL
EXTRAORDINARY

by **Robert Leo Odom**

87-1401

ISRAELITE HERITAGE INSTITUTE
P.O. BOX 1368
BRONX, NEW YORK 10475

Dedicated to my wife, Martha M. Odom,
who has helped in the preparation of this book.

CONTENTS

ABBREVIATIONS

BT	=	*Babylonian Talmud*
B.C.E.	=	Before the Common Era (B.C. = Before Christ)
C.E.	=	The Common Era (A.D. = Year of the Lord).
HUP	=	Harvard University Press
JT	=	*Jerusalem Talmud*
MTT	=	*Minor Tractates of the Talmud*
R.	=	Rabbi
JPS	=	Jewish Publication Society

INTRODUCTION

IT WAS a delightful and welcome surprise to me when I read Edward Hughes' article "Unearthing the Secrets of a Forgotten Kingdom" in *Reader's Digest* of June, 1978. In December of the same year *National Geographic* contained an article entitled "Ebla: Splendor of an Unknown Empire," by Howard LaFay, which was well illustrated with photographs of wonderful things discovered while uncovering the ancient city of Ebla, which had lain buried beneath the sands of the mound Tell Mardikh, situated about 35 miles southwest of the Syrian city of Aleppo.

Later in 1981, Doubleday and Company of Garden City, N.Y., published two books written by the leading men of the archaeological team that made the discovery possible. On the jacket of the book *Ebla: An Empire Rediscovered* the reader is told that it is written by Paolo Matthiae, a "brilliant young archaeologist," whose excavations on Tell Mardikh revealed the remains of a great city that was burned down more than 4000 years ago.

Another volume published by the same company in the same year was written by Giovanni Pettinato and entitled *The Archives of Ebla: an Empire Inscribed in Clay.* The author led out in transliterating and translating the many tablets brought out by the Ebla dig.

The most important find among the ruins of Ebla, which is said to have flourished in the twenty-third century B.C.E., was the royal library of the king of that ancient city. The excavators brought to light more than 15,000 clay tablets and fragments, written in cuneiform script.

The report states that Ebla was conquered by the Assyrians before 2300 B.C.E., and was later destroyed by Ashurnasirpal II, king of Assyria, in 2250 B.C.E.

The most delightful result of the archaeological work in uncovering that ancient city of Ebla is the fact that it throws great

Light on the history of the land that was so familiar to the patriarchs Abraham, Isaac, and Jacob. Abraham and Sarah lived in Ur of Chaldea and later in Haran before they migrated to the land of Canaan. Isaac's wife was born and grew up in Haran. Jacob spent 20 years of his life there, and it was there that he got his wives. Eleven of his 12 sons, and also his daughter Dinah, were born there.

Furthermore, such Semitic names as Adam, Abraham, Esau, Saul, David, Micaiah, and Jonah were found in the documents brought to light from the ruins of Ebla. Also, *Il* and *Ya,* equivalents of the Hebrew terms *El* and *Yah,* meaning "God" and "Lord" were used there in reference to the Deity. However, the evidence shows that there was considerable mingling of the worship of heathen gods with that of the true God in vogue in that region,[1] which corroborates the testimony of the Bible concerning the religious trends in Mesopotamia in the days of Abraham, Isaac, and Jacob.

Too, the two books mentioned above concerning Ebla reveal some interesting facts about the lunar calendation used by the people of Ebla. Interesting also is the fact that the reports on Ebla mention the creation story, and the discovery of a portion of a bilingual dictionary, which is of much value in interpreting those ancient tablets. Especially surprising is the fact that the name of the most important angel mentioned in the Holy Scriptures is also found in the Ebla tablets. He is the subject of this book, *Israel's Angel Extraordinary.*

FOOTNOTES AND REFERENCES

1. Genesis 31:19, 30-34; Joshua 24:15.

Chapter 1

"WHO IS LIKE GOD"

TO ME, a devoted worshiper of the God of Israel and a firm believer in the revelation of divine truth which He entrusted to His chosen people to share with the rest of the world, the most pleasant surprise found in the ruins of Ebla is the name of Israel's Angel extraordinary. Our attention is called to this by Howard LaFay, in his excellent article, "Ebla, Splendor of an Unknown Empire," in the *National Geographic* of December, 1978. He has pointed out that "in Ebla we find a man named Mi-ka-il (Who is like God?)—the modern Michael, of course," etc.[1]

And Giovanni Pettinato also, in his scholarly volume *The Archives of Ebla,* lists a number of personal names which had special significance in the religious life of the people of Ebla. One of them is "Mi-ka-il/ia—Who is like Il/Ya?"[2]

That term *"Mikail"* in the Semitic language of the Eblaites corresponds to "Michael" in the English version of the Holy Scriptures.

The name Michael is mentioned three times in the Book of Daniel,[3] which was written in the sixth century B.C.E. George Foot Moore, a scholarly convert to Judaism and a professor of the History of Religion at Harvard University, has made this thought-provoking remark:

"The author of the Book of Daniel does not introduce the names of Gabriel and Michael as if they were something new; on the contrary he assumes that both the names and the functions of these angels were familiar," etc.[4]

Israelite Men Named Michael

Dr. Moore is correct in saying that the name Michael was not "something new" in Daniel's time. It was a religiously cherished name. During the long period of nearly 1000 years from Moses to Daniel at least ten different men are mentioned in Holy Writ as having been given the name Michael. And during the 2½ millenniums since Daniel wrote, many men have been called Michael in other lands and languages.

Moses records that the man chosen from the tribe of Asher and sent as one of the 12 spies to the land of Canaan was "Sethur the son of Michael." Numbers 13:13.[5] He was a prominent leader of his tribe. Verses 2 and 3. Inasmuch as it was in the second year of the exodus of Israel from Egypt that those spies were sent into Canaan, this means that Sethur's father Michael was born and given that name at least 50 years or more before they left the land of Pharaohs. It would be interesting to know what led his parents to give him that significantly religious name. Nine other Hebrew men were mentioned as having that name during the period from the exodus from Egypt to the building of the second Temple in Jerusalem.[6] We may well believe that a great many other Jewish men not mentioned in the Scriptures also had that name Michael during those centuries.

But the notable person mentioned by the seer Daniel was a celestial being of very great rank and importance. Note particularly that in Daniel 10:13 the angel Gabriel states that Michael is "one of the chief princes."

The angel Gabriel is not mentioned by name elsewhere in the Hebrew Scriptures than in the Book of Daniel. He appears to be inferior in rank to Michael, whom he calls "the great prince [ha-sar ha-gadol] who standeth for the children of thy people." Daniel 12:1. Elsewhere he is called "one of the chief princes [ha-sarim ha ri'shonim]." Daniel 10:13.

One Palestinian haggadist of Talmudic status has taught: "Greater is [the achievement] ascribed to Michael than that ascribed to Gabriel."[7]

It has been well said: "Michael and Gabriel are the most prominent of all the angels and are often mentioned as cooperating in a task. . . . Michael is even superior to Gabriel in rank (Ber. 4b)."[8]

Michael's Name

Michael's name is an interesting one. It means "Who Is Like God." It is formed of three Hebrew words combined in this manner: *Mi* (Who)- *ka* (like)- *El* (God), and can be transliterated as *Mi-ka-El*. One Jewish reference work explains it thus:

"Michael (Heb. lit. 'Who is like unto God.'): the prince of angels, according to Dan. 10:13. As the archangel nearest to God he is the chief Divine messenger and executes God's judgments."[9]

The rabbis explained the name this way: "Why was his name called Michael *(Mi ka-el)*? When Israel crossed the Red Sea Moses began to chant, *Who* (mi) *is like unto Thee,* etc. (Ex. xv.11); and when he completed the Torah he said, *There is none like unto God* (ka-el), O Jeshurun (Deut. xxxiii, 26). From the two expressions *'mi (who) is like unto Thee'* and *'none* ka'el *(like unto God)'* you obtain the combination *mi ka'el*."[10]

In the Hebrew idiom the present tense verb "is" is implied, as is customary in some other languages. When the American Indian pointed to a large fellow and said, "He big man," he meant "He is a big man."

Angel Messengers

During the centuries since the Holy Scriptures were penned much has been written about Michael by religious writers. Some of it is fanciful and of little value. Nevertheless, some things written about him are worthy of our consideration.

To appreciate more fully the mission of Michael in the history of our world, certain facts ought to be kept in mind. First, that he is sometimes referred to as an angel, and again as an archangel. In the Hebrew text of the Sacred Scriptures the noun *mal'ak* is used 213 times, and is variously rendered into English as "angel" 11 times, "messenger" 98 times, and "ambassador" 4 times. The term simply means "one sent." It is derived from the Hebrew root *l'k* (or *l'ak*), which is not used in Holy Writ, according to Hebrew scholars.

When the Hebrew text of the Sacred Scriptures was translated into Greek in the third century B.C.E., *mal'ak* was rendered as *aggelos,* from which we get our English word "angel," which also means "one sent as a messenger." That is its primary meaning.

However, the use of the Hebrew term *mal'ak* and its corresponding Greek equivalent *aggelos* are not restricted in meaning solely to celestial beings. They are also used in reference to human beings. For example, Moses has recorded that Balak, king of Moab, "sent messengers [mal'akim] unto Balaam," an apostate prophet of Peor, to ask him to curse Israel. Numbers 22:5. And who were those *mal'akim* (messengers)? The record states that they were "the elders of Moab and the elders of Midian," who were human beings. Verse 7.

Before he began the seige of Jericho, Joshua "sent out of Shittim two spies secretly," to the city. Joshua 2:1. After the Israelites had taken Jericho, Joshua commanded his troops to spare the life of Rahab and her family "because she hid the messengers [*ha-mal'akim*] that we sent." Joshua 6:17. Elsewhere in the story of that event it is stated clearly that those "messengers" *(mal'akim)* were men.[11]

Several hundred years later, David sent 10 young men to Nabal, a wealthy man whose shepherds he had protected, to request of him provisions for himself and his men. Those "ten young men" are twice referred to as "messengers *[mal'akim]*" in that story. They, too, were *human* messengers.[12]

Later Necho, king of Egypt, "sent ambassadors [*mal'akim*]" to Josiah, king of Judah. 2 Chronicles 35:20, 21. In this account, as also in the other, the Greek text (LXX) calls those messengers *aggelos.*

Thus it is obvious that in Holy Writ the term *mal'ak* simply means a person sent as an ambassador or messenger, and that the person so sent may be a celestial being in some cases, and in other cases a human being.

Michael and Gabriel

A modern Jewish reference work correctly states: "There is reference only to the two Biblical angels Michael and Gabriel."[13] That is, in the Hebrew text only two are mentioned *by name,* and that only in the Book of Daniel.

In the post-Biblical period they were regarded by many Jewish rabbis as "the kings of the angels."[14]

Michael, the Archangel

Michael, as the archangel—that is, as ruler or king of the holy angels—was held in very high esteem in Israel of long ago. For example, he is referred to as "Michael the Archangel" in the Talmudic writings.[15] In one tractate he is referred to as "Michael the great Prince."[16] An editorial footnote to that statement explains that he is "the Archangel."[17]

A well known reference work aptly remarks: "It is quite natural that, owing to his position with regard to the Jews, Michael should be represented in the Haggadah as the most prominent of the archangels."[18]

Michael, the Great Prince

In Holy Writ this remarkable celestial being is called "Michael, one of the chief princes." Daniel 10:13. Also, "Michael your prince." Verse 21. And again he is referred to as "Michael . . . the great prince who standeth for the children of thy people." Daniel 12:1. Thus he is divinely declared to stand in special relationship to God's people on earth. That is why Michael has been held in very high esteem among God's people since ancient times.

The Hebrew noun *sar* rendered as "prince" in these passages in the Book of Daniel signifies a person of high rank and authority. It is used 13 times by Daniel in reference to important persons, including the rulers of the Persian and Greek empires, as well as those of the Kingdom of Judah.[19] In the rest of the Holy Scriptures it is similarly used to denote persons of great importance.

One of the leading Christian Jews of the first century C.E. likewise speaks of "Michael the archangel" (Jude 9), which indicates that Michael was a celestial being held in high esteem long after Daniel's time.

The noun *sar* appears 419 times in the Hebrew text of the Holy Scriptures. It is translated into English as "prince" more than 200 times. Hence he is referred to as, "Michael, the angel-prince of Jerusalem."[20]

Tutelary Prince of Israel

The term "tutelary" means guardian and teacher. Michael held a place of great importance in relation to ancient Israel. The angel who instructed Daniel referred to him as "Michael . . . the great Prince who standeth for the children of thy people," (Daniel 12:1), and as "your prince" (Daniel 10:21). Hence this Scripture passage is cited by a well known Jewish reference work as meaning that Michael "is also represented as the tutelary [guiding or guardian] prince of Israel."[21]

Israel's Guardian Angel

It is interesting to note that in their high regard for Michael and his princely role, rabbinical writers have referred to him as Israel's Guardian Angel.

A Talmudic tractate speaks of him as "Michael, the great Prince."[22] The editorial footnote explains that "Michael is Israel's guardian Angel."[23]

He is called also "the Custodian of Israel" in some of the ancient rabbinical writings. However, the Holy Scriptures clearly show that the Lord did not defend Israel in times of her apostasy but reproved her for her evildoing.

We are informed also that "Michael, the guardian angel of Israel, ranks above the rest. He is one of the chief princes, his name signifying 'who is like God?' being expressive of God's greatness."[24]

A Midrashic statement on Psalm 134:1 calls him "Michael the great guardian angel."[25]

Another modern Jewish reference work tells us: "He is the viceroy of God, and the special defender of Israel."[26]

"According to Dan. 10:13, he [Michael] fought against the princes of the other nations, and in Dan. 12:1 he is to stand up and defend Israel in time of great trouble."[27]

One Jewish reference work says: "The Rabbis declare that Michael entered upon his role of defender at the time of the patriarchs."[28] There are many instances in Holy Writ showing that from the time of the patriarch Jacob and through the period of the judges and kings the Angel of the Lord defended Israel against her enemies on condition of her loyalty and obedience to Him. For instance, Michael is said to have smitten 185,000 men of the army of Sennacherib, king of Assyria, in a single night when they were about to attack Jerusalem.[29]

Michael "is the viceroy of God, and the special defender of Israel."[30] "He is the medium for transmission of the Law to Moses and Israel."[31]

"Michael is credited also with having guided Israel safely through the wilderness, annihilating the army of Sennacherib, and saving the three Hebrew youths from the fiery furnace of Nebuchadnezzar."[32]

The amazing story of the ministry of holy angels sent by God to protect and help his people, as recorded in the Holy Scriptures, is a wonderful theme for study. That of Michael, as God's Angel extraordinary, deserves much more study than most of us imagine.

FOOTNOTES AND REFERENCES

1. Pages 737, 740.
2. Pages 261, 276.
3. Daniel 10:13, 21; 12:1.
4. George Foot Moore, *Judaism in the First Centuries of the Christian Era,* vol. 1, p. 403.
5. *The Holy Scriptures,* Jewish Publication Society of America (JPS). (This version is used unless otherwise specified.)
6. 1 Chronicles 5:13, 14; 6:25 (40); 7:3; 8:16; 12:21; 27:18; 2 Chronicles 21:2: Ezra 8:8.
7. BT *Berakoth* 4b (p. 15).
8. A. Cohen, *Everyman's Talmud,* p. 50.
9. *The Standard Jewish Encyclopedia,* page 134, art. "Messiah."

10. *Midrash Rabbah* on Numbers, chap. 2, sect. 10 (vol. 1, p. 39). See also: *Midrash Rabbah* on Exodus, chap. 29, sect. 2, (p. 338); *The Midrash on Psalms* 17:3 (vol. 1, p. 205); *Pesikta Rabbati*, Piska 46, sect. 3 (vol. 2, p. 792).

11. Joshua 2:1-5, 9, 14, 17, 23.

12. 1 Samuel 25:5, 10, 14, 42.

13. *Encyclopedia Judaica,* vol. 15, p. 775.

14. *Midrash Rabbah* on Ecclesiastes 11, sect. 2 (p. 246); on Numbers 11, sect. 3 (vol. 1, p. 419); Pesikta Rabbati, Piska 15, sect. 3 (vol. 1, p. 310); on Song of Songs chap. 3, sect. 7, part. 5 (p. 164) plus note 1; chap. 8, sect. 11, part 2 (page 319).

15. BT *Hullin* 40a (page 215).

16. BT *Abodah Zarah* 42b (p. 211).

17. *Ibid.,* footnote no. 6.

18. *The Jewish Encyclopedia,* vol. 8, page 537 col. 2, art. "Michael."

19. Daniel 9:6, 8; 10:13, 20.

20. Targum on the Psalms, Psalm 137, sects, 7 & 8. See *The Jewish Encyclopedia,* vol. 1, p. 594, col. 2.

21. *Ibid,* vol. 8, p. 535, col. 2, art. "Michael."

22. BT *Hagigah* 12b (p. 70).

23. *Ibid.,* Footnote no. 1; cf. Daniel 12:1 and BT *Yoma* 77a (p. 374). See also *Menahoth* 110a, with footnote no. 5 (p. 680).

24. *The Jewish Encyclopedia,* vol. 1, p. 589, col. 2.

25. *The Midrash on Psalms* 134. 1 (vol. 2, p. 321). See also: Pesikta Rabbati 21.1 (vol. 1, p. 32, note. 60); 30.4 (vol. 2, p. 596); 15.3 (vol. 1, p. 310); *The Jewish Encyclopedia,* vol. 9, page 202, col. 1.

26. *The Universal Jewish Encyclopedia,* vol. 7, page 529, col. 2.

27. *Ibid.*

28. *The Jewish Encyclopedia,* vol. 8, page 536, col. 1.

29. See 2 Kings 19:35; Isaiah 37:36,37; 2 Chronicles 32:21. *Midrash Rabbah* on Exodus, chap. 18, sect. 5 (pages 220, 221).

30. *The Universal Jewish Encyclopedia,* vol. 7, page 529, col. 2.

31. *Ibid.*

32. *Ibid.*

Chapter 2

MICHAEL AND ABRAHAM

WHEN the patriarch Abraham chose to establish his home among the terebinths at Mamre, which is also called Hebron, he did not imagine what distinguished visitors would be his guests there. The story of what happened begins this way:

"And the LORD [YHWH] appeared unto him by the terebinths of Mamre, as he sat in the tent door in the heat of the day; (2) and he lifted up his eyes and looked, and, lo, three men stood over against him; and when he saw them, he ran to meet them from the tent door, and bowed down to the earth, (3) and said: 'My lord, if now I have found favour in thy sight, pass not away, I pray thee, from thy servant. (4) Let now a little water be fetched, and wash your feet, and recline yourselves under the tree. (5) And I will fetch a morsel of bread, and stay ye your heart; after that ye shall pass on; forasmuch as ye are come to your servant.' And they said: 'So do, as thou hast said.' "; Genesis 18:1-5.

When Moses wrote those words, little did he think that there would be some controversy over them during the first and second millenniums C.E. For example, who were the "three men" mentioned in verse 2? Was "the LORD (YHWH)" mentioned in the first verse one of them? A few Jewish scholars have supposed that there were four persons—God and three angels.[1]

The evidence, however, indicates that there were only three— the LORD and two angels. When they left Abraham's home, the LORD paused to tell him of His intention to destroy Sodom. Then the other two heavenly visitors "turned from thence, and went toward Sodom; but Abraham stood yet before the LORD," to plead for the righteous persons in that wicked city. Then "the LORD went His way, as soon as He had left off speaking to Abraham; and Abraham returned unto his place." Verses 22-33.

The sacred narrative goes on to say that "the two angels came to Sodom at even." Genesis 19:1. This indicates that two of the three celestial beings who, in the guise of men, had visited Abraham at Mamre, were angels.

The rest of the narrative in chapter 19 makes that fact quite clear. Nowhere in chapters 18 and 19 does the narrative speak of three angels. It specifically mentions "two angels."

LORD and "Lord"

It is surprising that very few readers of the Holy Scriptures in English note the fact that throughout the Sacred Writings the Deity is often referred to by the name "Lord," printed with a capital "L" and three small letters "ord," while in many more instances He is mentioned in print as "LORD," with the large capital "L" and three small capital letters "ORD." Why?

This is done because two different Hebrew words used in reference to the Deity are translated into English as "Lord." One of them is *'Adon* and the other is *YHWH* (mistakenly rendered as "Jehovah" in some English versions), which is now known to have been anciently pronounced as *Yahweh.* In order that English readers might know the difference, the translators made a rule, in reference to the Deity, to render *'Adon* as "Lord," and to render *YHWH* as either "LORD" or "GOD." Frequently God is referred to as *'Adonai YHWH,* and for this reason this combination is rendered as "Lord GOD."

In Genesis 18

It is evident, then, in the light of the Mosaic record concerning the "three men" who, in the guise of wayfarers, visited Abraham at Mamre and went from there to Sodom, as recorded in Genesis 18 and 19, that (1) they were three celestial beings; (2) the chief among them was referred to at first as "lord" in verse 3; and (3) the other two were simply referred to as "two angels." Genesis 19:1.

If it is assumed that Abraham did not recognize *at first* that his wayfaring guests were celestial beings, and supposed them

20

to be men, it would be reasonable to assume also that the patriarch would politely address their chief as "my lord." Also, that when he became aware of the chief guest's true identity, he would then reverently address Him as "the Lord" and "the Judge of all the earth." Verse 25. In this light, the translators may seem to be justified in rendering *'adonai* as "lord" in verse 3.

Interesting is the fact that the word "God" is not used in chapter 18.

In verse 3 the Hebrew text reads "Adonai," which is rendered as "lord" in the JPS version. However, in the English texts prepared by Isaac Leeser and Alexander Harkavy the Hebrew noun is rendered as "Lord," as it is done in the KJV.

Note, too, the fact that Abraham addresses the same chief celestial visitor as *'Adonai* in verses 27, 30, 31, and 32; and that the translators render it as "Lord" (with a capital "L") in all these four instances. Besides, the patriarch addresses Him reverently as "the Judge of all the earth" in verse 25; Moses refers to Him as "the LORD *[YHWH]*" in verses 1, 13, 17, 20, 22, 26, and 33; and the translators have rendered the Tetragrammaton *(YHWH)* as "LORD" (with a capital "L" and three small capital letters "ORD") without hesitation.

In Talmudic Works

It is not surprising that in post Biblical times, when the people of Israel were widely scattered and divided into several different religious communities, there should be some disagreement of opinion among them in matters of doctrine. In any case, a doctrine that accords with both the Holy Scriptures and common sense is an acceptable one. On this particular point of doctrine a modern reference work has said:

"Three angels in human guise were hospitably entertained by Abraham in Mamre, where the Lord again foretold Isaac's birth, and when Sarah doubted the promise, the Lord himself appeared and renewed it (Gen. xviii. 1-15).

"In recognition of Abraham's piety the Lord now acquainted him with His intention to destroy Sodom and Gomorrah on account of their wickedness; but, after several appeals from Abraham, He promised that Sodom should be spared if ten righteous men could be found therein (*ib.* xviii 17-32."[2]

Is the Holy One the celestial being referred to as "the LORD" throughout Genesis 18?

In one Talmudic tractate we find it said concerning Abraham: "So he himself went out, and saw the Holy One, blessed be He, standing at the door; thus it is written, *Pass not away, I pray thee, from thy servant.*"[3]

Furthermore, in an editorial footnote to that statement it is said: "He [Abraham] called himself '*thy servant,*' because he was speaking to God."[4]

In an article entitled 'Names of God," a modern reference work points its readers to Genesis 18:3, as follows: "Adonai sometimes refers to a distinguished person (comp. Gen. xviii.3)."[5] Also: "It was, probably, at first Adoni ('My Lord') or Adonai ('My Lord,' plural of Majesty), and later assumed this form, as a proper name, to distinguish it from other uses of the same word."[6]

In another Talmudic work we are told: "All the Names mentioned in Scripture in connection with Abraham are sacred, except this which is secular: it is said: *And he said, 'My lord, if now I have found favour in thy sight'.* Hanina, the son of R. Joshua's brother, and R. Eleazar b. Azariah in the name of R. Eliezer of Modin, said, this also is sacred."[7] An editorial footnote to that passage says concerning Abraham: "He was addressing the Lord."[8] That is a remarkable statement insofar as the identity of the chief visitor is concerned. R. Eleazar b. Azariah was a very popular and influential mishnaic scholar of the first century C.E.[9]

Other Talmudic Statements

Another Talmudic work says: "All nouns in the Torah [signifying God] that are mentioned in connection with Abraham are sacred except the first. R. Hanina the son of R. Joshua's brother holds that it is sacred."[10] A footnote to that statement says: "In his opinion *my lord* was addressed to God."[11]

A similar statement reads: "All the names [signifying God] mentioned in connection with Abraham are sacred, except one which is secular, viz. where it is stated, *And he said: My lord, if now I have found favor in thy sight.* Others say that it is sacred."[12] A footnote says: "*My Lord* was addressed to God."[13]

In reference to the heavenly visitor who speaks in Genesis 18:21, another Talmudic work attributes to the "Divine Presence" this statement: "I will go down now, and see whether they have done altogether according to the cry of it. (Gen. 18:21)."[14]

In the Midrashic Writings

A midrashic work states concerning Abraham: "On which occasion did he act with special courtesy?—When he said: *My Lord . . . pass not away, I pray Thee, from Thy servant . . .* and he stood by them under the tree whilst they ate (Gen. XVIII, 3,8)."[15] An editorial footnote says in reference to the phrase "My Lord" in verse 3: "With a capital L, so understood by the Midrash. The Massorah too designates Adonai here as 'holy', i.e. referring to God."[16]

Another Midrashic work has this to say: "Abraham called himself a servant, for he said, *My Lord . . . pass not away, I pray Thee, from Thy servant* (Gen. 18:3)."[17]

"When did Abraham go to God with singleness of heart? When he said: *My Lord, if now I have found favor in Thy sight, pass not away, I pray Thee, from Thy servant* (Gen. 18:3)."[18]

Note the capital "L" in "Lord" in those passages, which shows belief that the celestial visitor referred to was the Holy One of Israel.

Abraham "Sat"

The Sacred Record says that the patriarch "sat in the tent door in the heat of the day." Genesis 18:1.

A very few have interpreted those words to mean that Abraham "sat in the tent door" to study and pray.[19]

Abraham Sick and Sore from Circumcision?

A more popular view has been that Abraham was sick and sore from his having been circumcised, as mentioned in Genesis 17. While the Targum of Onkelos makes no mention of his being sick and in pain from circumcision, both the Targum of Jerusalem and that of Palestine say that he was ill from the pain of circumcision.

A Talmudic tractate says: *"And the Lord appeared unto him in the plains of Mamre: and he sat in the tent door in the heat of the day* [Gen. 18:1]. What is meant by *'in the heat of the day'*?— R. Hama son of R. Hanina said: It was the third day from Abraham's circumcision, and the Holy One, blessed be He, came to enquire after Abraham's health; [moreover,] he drew the sun out of its sheath, so that the righteous man [sc. Abraham] should not be troubled with wayfarers. He sent Eliezer out [to seek travelers], but he found none. Said he, 'I do not believe thee'. (Hence they say there—sc. in Palestine—slaves are not to be believed.) So he himself went out, and saw the Holy One, blessed be He, standing at the door; thus it is written, *Pass not away, I pray thee, from they servant* (Gen. XVIII.3). But on seeing him tying and untying [the bandages of his circumcision], He said, 'It is not well that I stand here'; hence it is written, *And he lifted up his eyes and looked, and lo, three men stood by him, and when he saw them, he ran to meet them:'* at first they came and stood over him, but when they saw him in pain, they said, 'It is not seemly to stand here.' "[20]

Similar statements are found in other Talmudic tractates.[21]

Chapter 18 of Genesis says nothing whatever of Abraham being sore and ill from having been circumcised, or that he was swathed in bandages because of it when the celestial visitors came to him. It is true that some time prior to this he was circumcised, as recorded in Genesis 17:10-27, with other male members of his household, when he was 99 years old. We learn from Genesis 17:17; 18:12; 21:1-7 that Isaac, the promised son, was born in the 100th year of Abraham's life. But the notion that it was on the third day after his circumcision, and that he was sick and sore from it, and that he was still swathed in bandages at the time of the visit by the heavenly guests is nowhere supported by Holy Writ.

The evidence appears to show that such was not Abraham's physical condition at that time. It is clearly stated that when he saw the wayfarers approaching his place, "he *ran* to meet them from the tent door, and bowed down to the earth." Genesis 18:2. Also that "Abraham *ran* unto the herd, and fetched a calf" to be killed and cooked for the meal. Likewise "he hastened to dress it." Verse 7. This makes it quite obvious that he was then a well and able man in his 99th year of life. Just how long this occurred after his circumcision is not stated. If he had been too sore to move about, he could easily have bidden one of his servants to catch the calf.

It is amazing how some of Israel's religious teachers of long ago have presumed to add to the Mosaic record a lot of things that he never said. For example, concerning the meal that Abraham and Sarah prepared for their guests at the time mentioned in Genesis 18, it is said; "See how much Abraham prepared for the ministering angels—he went and prepared for them three oxen and nine measures of fine flour! Whence do we know that he prepared for them nine measures of fine flour? For it is stated, *And Abraham hastened into the tent unto Sarah, and said: Make ready quickly three measures of fine meal.* Now the word *three* signifies literally what it says; *fine* also implies three making six; and *meal* implies a further three, making nine in all. And whence do we know that he prepared for them three oxen? for it is stated, *And Abraham ran unto the herd and fetched a calf tender [and good].* Now the word *herd* implies one, *calf* implies another making two, and *tender* implies a third, thus making three in all. Some say that the word *good* implies a fourth."[22]

That shows that we must stay close to the Written Word of God—the Holy Scriptures—and be careful not to accept any religious teaching that does not agree with what the God of Israel has said through His prophets.

Michael, the Chief Visitor

According to Jewish religious teaching, the three celestial visitors at the home of Abraham and Sarah in Mamre (Hebron), as recorded in Genesis 18, were Michael, Gabriel, and Raphael. As stated in the first chapter of this book, Michael is the archangel mentioned in Daniel 10:13,21; 12:1. Gabriel, who is an angel of high rank associated with Michael, is mentioned in Daniel 8:16; 9:21. The Holy Scriptures do not mention any angel by the name of Raphael; but a Levite man having that name is mentioned in 1 Chronicles 26:7.

The conversation of the guests at Abraham's home (as recorded in Genesis 18:9-15) concerning Sarah who was inside the tent and apparently not visible to them, indicates that they were much better informed about her than he had imagined. How did they know her name? Why were they interested particularly in her and her future?

A modern reference work aptly informs its readers concerning Michael: "He announced to Sarah that she would bear a son (comp. Gen. xviii. 10); and he rescued Lot at the destruction of Sodom (B.M. 86b; comp. Gen. R. 1. 2)."[23]

A Talmudic writer says concerning the three heavenly visitors at Abraham's home: "Who were the three men?—Michael, Gabriel, and Raphael. Michael came to bring the tidings to Sarah [of Isaac's birth]."[24]

In Midrashic Writings

In the Midrashic texts of long ago there are several statements in which the chief of the heavenly guests of Abraham at Mamre is said to be Michael. It is written that Abraham said: MY LORD, IF NOW I HAVE FOUND FAVOUR IN THY SIGHT (XVIII, 3). R. Hiyya taught: He said this to the greatest of them, viz. Michael.[25]

Note particularly that in this instance the word is "Lord" and not "lord," in this obvious reference to Gen. 18:3. That is a very significant concept of Michael, whose name means "Who Is Like God," as taught by R. Hiyya.[26]

In another Midrashic work we read: "R. Berekiah said on the verse, *'I the Lord have spoken and done it':* Where did He speak it?—At the set time I will return unto thee . . . and Sarah *shall have a son* (Gen. XVIII, 14). *'And I have done it'*—AND THE LORD DID UNTO SARAH AS HE HAD SPOKEN."[27] That statement is interesting because it maintains that the celestial being who made the promise concerning Sarah, as recorded in Gen. 18:14, was "the Lord," the same Holy One mentioned in Gen. 21:1.

It is said concerning Abraham: "The Holy One, blessed be He, spake to him: 'You said, *And I will fetch a morsel of bread* (Gen. XVIII, 5)."[28] That statement makes it very clear that the writer believed that the heavenly guest who spoke to the patriarch in Genesis 18:5 was the Holy One of Israel. It is remarkable and especially noteworthy that some of Israel's teachers believed and taught that the chief of the three heavenly guests of Abraham at Mamre was Michael, and that he was a divine person.

Especially interesting is the following Midrashic statement: "R. Judah b. R. Simon and R. Johanan in the name of R. Eleazar b. Simon said: The Holy One, blessed be He, never spoke directly with a woman save with that righteous woman [viz. Sarah], and that too was due to a particular cause. R. Abba b. Kahana said in R. Biryi's name: And what a roundabout way He went in order to speak with her! As it is written, *And He said; Nay; but thou didst laugh* (Gen. XVIII, 15)."[29]

In that case, as we have noted in others, the heavenly guest who spoke to Sarah in Genesis 18:15 was the Holy One of Israel.

FOOTNOTES AND REFERENCES

1. See BT *Shabbath* 127a (page 632) and footnote no. 4; MTT *Kallah Rabbathi* 54a, chap. 7 (vol. 2, page 487); *Derek 'Erez Rabbah* 56a, chap. 4. sect. 2 (vol. 2, page 546).

2. *The Jewish Encyclopedia,* vol. 1, page 84, cols. 1, 2.

3. BT *Baba Mezia* 86b (page 499).

4. *Ibid.,* footnote no. 12.

5. *The Jewish Encyclopedia,* vol. 9, page 163, col. 2.

6. *Ibid.,* page 162, col. 1.

7. BT *Shebu'oth* 35b (page 205).

8. *Ibid.,* footnote no. 6.

9. *The Jewish Encyclopedia,* vol. 5, pages 97, 98.

10. MTT *Sefer Torah,* chap. 4, rule 6 (vol. 2, pages 640, 641).

11. *Ibid.,* footnote no. 24.

12. MTT *Soferim* 36b, chap. 4, rule 6 (vol. 1, page 228).

13. *Ibid.,* footnote no. 31.

14. MTT *'Aboth d'Rabbi Nathan,* 30b, chap. 34, sect. 6 (vol. 1, page 167). The same is said in *Pirke de R. Eliezer,* chap. 25, page 179.

15. *Midrash Rabbah* on Leviticus, chap. 11, sect. 5 (page. 139).

16. *Ibid.,* footnote no. 3. The Massorah is the system which represents the work of the Jewish scholars who, in the period from 800 to 100 C.E. supplied the traditional vowel-points for the Bible text to insure that it might be read correctly. In order that the proper distinction might be made in reading aloud the Hebrew word *'adon* in its plural form, two different vowels were provided for the last syllable. If reference is made to the Deity as "Lord," then that syllable would be marked with the vowel sign $\overline{\tau}$, which corresponds to the sound of the letter "a" as in the English word "all." But if the reference is to angels or to men as "lords," the vowel sign for the last syllable of the word would be $\div$, which corresponds to the "a" as in the English word "class." That distinction is made in the printed text of our Hebrew Bibles. This is the reason why, as indicated above, that the Massorah has given to the second syllable of the Hebrew word *'Adonai* (the plural form) in Genesis 18:3.

17. *The Midrash on Psalms,* Psalm 18, sect. 4 (vol. 1, page 231).

18. *Ibid.,* sect. 22 (vol. 1, pages 250, 251).

19. See *Pesikta Rabbati,* piska 15, sect. 9 (vol. 1, page 318).

20. BT *Baba Mezia* 86b, (pages 499, 500).

21. See BT *Sotah* 14a (pages 72, 73); MTT *Kallah Rabbathi* 54a, chap. 7 (vol. 2, pages 487, 489); *Derek 'Erez Rabbah* 56b, chap. 4, sect. 2 (vol. 2, page 546). See also *Midrash Rabbah* on Numbers, chap. 11, sect. 2 (vol. 1, pages 414, 415); on Ecclesiastes, chap. 7, sect. 1, part 1 (page 174); *The Midrash on Psalms* Psalm 25, sect. 11 (vol. 1, page 354); *Pirke de R. Eliezer,* chap. 29 (page 205).

22. MTT *'Aboth D'Rabbi Nathan* 23b, chap. 13, sect. 3 (vol. 1, pages 81, 82).

23. *The Jewish Encyclopedia,* vol. 8, page 536, col. 1.

24. BT *Baba Mezia* 86a (p. 500). The same thing is taught in *The Jewish Encyclopedia,* vol. 1, page 588, col. 1, page 593 col. 2; vol. 10, page 318, col. 1; BT *Yoma* 37a (page 172); MTT *Kallah Rabbathi,* chap. 7, baraitha 54a (vol. 2, pages 487, 489); *Derek 'Eretz Rabbah* 56b, chap. 4, sect. 2 (vol. 2, pages 546, 547).
25. *Midrash Rabbah* on Genesis 48, sect. 10 (vol. 1, page 411).
26. R. Hiyya bar Abba was a Palestinian amora of priestly descent who flourished at the end of the third century C.E. *The Jewish Encyclopedia,* vol. 6, page 430, col. 1.
27. *Midrash Rabbah* on Genesis, chap. 53, sect. 1 (vol. 1, page 461).
28. *Ibid.,* on Ecclesiastes, chap. 11, sect. 1, part 1 (page 288).
29. *Ibid.,* on Genesis, chap. 20, sect. 6 (vol. 1, pages 163, 164).

Chapter 3

MICHAEL AT SODOM

WHEN THE three celestial visitors in the guise of men left Mamre Abraham accompanied them a short distance toward Sodom. The Sacred Record states that when they reached a certain point, the LORD said: "Shall I hide from Abraham that which I am doing?" Genesis 18:16, 17.

They stopped and the Lord revealed to the patriarch His purpose concerning Sodom. Verses 17-21. Here the chief among the three heavenly guests of Abraham is said to be "the LORD" (YHWH), and the patriarch addressed Him as "the Judge of all the earth" in verse 25. While the Holy One was talking to Abraham about that wicked city, the other two heavenly beings "went toward Sodom." Verse 22. When His conversation with Abraham ended, "the LORD went His way." Verse 33.

The two angels in the guise of men arrived at Sodom at even. A Midrashic treatise states twice that those two angels were Gabriel and Raphael. The Mosaic record does not reveal their names.[1] They were invited to spend the night at the home of Lot, the nephew of Abraham. It was a bad night for them because a mob of wicked men persisted in trying to break into the house to abuse them. Genesis 19:1-11. Lot's angelic guests smote the men with blindness, and told him that they had come by command of the LORD to destroy the city because of its wickedness. Verses 12-14.

When the morning dawned the angels urged Lot, his wife, and two daughters to leave the city immediately. When he lingered, they led them out by the hand.

It is written that when they were outside the city, "he said: Escape for thy life." Verse 17. In verse 18 Lot calls that celestial being "my lord." The Hebrew noun here rendered as "lord" is *'adonai,* which is translated as "lord" (with a capital "L")

31

when quoted in *Midrash Rabbah* to Genesis.[2] Note in that verse 17 the personal pronoun "he", singular in number, and which is not capitalized by the translators. It is used in obvious reference to a celestial person of high authority, as seen by his statement in verses 21 and 22, where he reveals that he is the one in charge of destroying the city, saying to Lot: "See, I have accepted thee concerning this thing also, that I will not overthrow the city of which thou hast spoken. Hasten thou, escape thither; for I cannot do any thing till thou be come thither." Verses 21, 22.

That statement in verse 17 quoted above, has been a baffling one to some of Israel's religious teachers. Concerning a rabbinical discussion about it long ago, we read: "A difficulty was raised: It is written, *'And it came to pass, when they had brought them forth'?* Read what follows, he replied; it is not written, 'And *they* said,' but AND *HE* SAID: ESCAPE FOR THY LIFE."[3]

In specific reference to Genesis 19:17-19, a Talmudic tractate says: "All the Names mentioned in connection with Lot are secular, except this which is sacred: it is said: *And Lot said unto them, 'Oh, not so, my Lord; behold now, thy servant hath found grace in thy sight, [and thou hast magnified thy mercy which thou hast shown unto me in saving my life]'* [Gen. XIX, 18, 19]—He in whose power it is to kill and to revive; that is, the Holy One, blessed be He."[4]

Who Is "He"?

When Lot and his daughters had left Sodom and entered Zoar, shortly after sunrise, "then the LORD caused to rain upon Sodom and upon Gomorrah brimstone and fire from the LORD out of heaven; and He overthrew those cities, and all the Plain, and all the inhabitants of the cities, and that which grew upon the ground." Verses 24, 25.

This verse 24 of Genesis 19 has been the subject of considerable discussion among rabbis of long ago, and it still is among some today,[5] because it speaks of *two different celestial Beings called*

"LORD," one of them causing fire to come down from the other in heaven to destroy Sodom. It is obvious that the first-mentioned "LORD" in this verse 24 was the same "LORD" who spoke with Abraham in chapter 18, implying that he would "destroy" the wicked Sodomites, as indicated in the conversation between Him and the patriarch, if He should find less than ten righteous persons there. Genesis 18:23-32.

The two angels who spent the night in Sodom informed Lot the next morning that "the LORD hath sent us to destroy it [the city of Sodom]." Genesis 19:13. Lot told his sons-in-law "the *LORD will destroy the city.*" Verse 14. In verses 17 and 21 that same celestial personage is introduced by the pronoun "he." We have noted already in verses 21 and 22 that the same celestial being of high authority speaks of Himself as personally directing the operation. This indicates that the speaker was invested with authority to destroy that wicked city. And in verses 24 and 25 it is said that "the LORD caused to rain upon Sodom and upon Gomorrah brimstone and fire from the LORD out of heaven; and He overthrew those cities," etc.

In the light of all this, it is obvious that the person referred to as "He" (with a capital "H") in verse 25 is the same one referred to as "he" in verses 17 to 21. Furthermore, we must conclude, also, that the same celestial person is the first one called "the LORD" in verse 24, who "caused to rain upon Sodom and upon Gomorrah brimstone and fire."

Diversity of Opinion

In the rabbinical writings of the distant past we find much diversity of opinion among them concerning the two celestial beings called "LORD" in Genesis 19:24. Some speak of them as two distinct persons. The translators of the Septuagint (LXX) text follow the Hebrew text in mentioning two separate persons called "LORD." So do others.[6]

The *Targum of Onkelos* on Genesis 19:24 mentions two persons called "LORD." The *Targum of Palestine* refers to one as "the Lord," and to the other as "the Word of the Lord." So does the *Targum of Jerusalem.*

Omissions

In quoting and discussing Genesis 19:24 some of the rabbis in the distant past omitted entirely the second "Lord" mentioned in the last part of that verse. For example, we read in one Talmudic tractate: "In the case of Sodom it is written, *And the Lord rained upon Sodom [and upon Gomorrah brimstone and fire],*" etc.[7]

Others construe the word "Lord" in the latter part of verse 24 to mean either "Himself" or "His Court."[8]

The phrase "from the Lord out of heaven" is made to read "from heaven" in some rabbinical texts, and in others it is left out entirely.[9]

The best policy would be to take God's Word at its face value and not presume to bend or twist it to fit our own wishes or preconceived ideas. For example, this is said in a Talmudic tractate: "A *Min* once said to R. Ishmael b. Jose: It is written, *Then the Lord caused to rain upon Sodom and Gomorrah brimstone and fire from the Lord* [Gen. 19:24]; but *from him* should have been written!"[10] (An apostate was called a *Min.*)

Michael

As some of the rabbis did in discussing the chief of the three visitors in Genesis 18, so in Genesis 19 he is regarded as Michael, the One "Who Is Like God." Therefore, he is the first one referred to as "Lord" in Genesis 19:24. In fact, a modern reference work states concerning Michael that "he rescued Lot at the destruction of Sodom (B.M. 86b; comp. Gen. R. 1.2)."[11]

One Talmudic tractate states concerning Gabriel: "Michael accompanied him to rescue Lot. [The Writ] supports this too, for it is written, *And he overthrew those cities* [Gen. 19:25], not, and *they* overthrew: this proves it."[12]

That is, while Michael was conversing with Abraham about the impending destruction of Sodom (Gen. 18:17-22), the other two angels proceeded to Sodom and arrived there "at even"

34

(Genesis 19:1). Michael joined them later at Sodom in time to give instructions to Lot before the city was destroyed. Verses 17-22.

The Holy One who appeared to Abraham at Mamre, as stated in Genesis 18, was the principal one of the three celestial visitors whom he entertained. Before Him, as "Judge of all the earth" (verse 25), the patriarch made intercession for the righteous persons in Sodom. That LORD who caused fire to come down from heaven to destroy Sodom after rescuing Lot, was Michael, whom we may rightly call Israel's Angel extraordinary.

FOOTNOTES AND REFERENCES

1. *Midrash Rabbah* on Genesis, chap. 50, sects. 2, 3 (vol. 1, pages 434, 435).
2. *Ibid.,* sect. 11 (page 441).
3. *Ibid.*
4. BT *Shebu'oth* 35b (pages 205, 206). This same thing is said in MTT *Soferim,* chap. 4, rule 7 (vol. 1, pages 228, 229), and footnotes 38 and 39; *Sefer Torah,* chap. 4, rule 7 (vol. 2, page 641).
5. In our own time it has been referred to by some as "a different, but glaring grammatical problem."—*Geshur,* vol. 7, 1979, pages 25, 26.
6. See *The Midrash on Psalms* 5.7 (vol. 1, page 87); 149.1 (vol. 2, page 379); *Pesikta Rabbati,* piska 42, sect. 3 (vol. 2, page 739).
7. BT *Sanhedrin* 104b (page 711).
8. See *Midrash Rabbah* on Genesis, chap. 51, sect. 2 (vol. 1, page 445).
9. For examples of this see: *Midrash Rabbah* on Exodus, chap. 25, sect. 1 (page 301); on Leviticus, chap. 4, sect. 1 (page 48); chap. 5, sect. 2 (page 62); chap. 7, sect. 6 (page 98);. on Numbers, chap. 11, sect. 7 (vol. 1, page 443); on Song of Songs, chap. 8, sect. 9, part 2 (page 312); on Ecclesiastes, chap. 2, sect. 1 (page 53); sect. 23, (page 71); *The Midrash on Psalms* 11.5 (vol. 1, page 162).
10. BT *Sanhedrin* 38b (page 246).
11. *The Jewish Encyclopedia,* vol. 8, page 536, col. 1.
12. BT *Baba Mezia* 86b (page 500).

Chapter 4

MICHAEL AND ISAAC

TO REVEAL the extent to which the patriarch would faithfully obey Him, "God did prove Abraham, and said unto him: 'Abraham'; and he said: 'Here am I.' And He said: 'Take now thy son, thine only son, whom thou lovest, even Isaac, and get thee into the land of Moriah; and offer him there for a burnt-offering.'" This Abraham promptly proceeded to do. When he had built there an altar and bound Isaac thereon, he took the knife to slay the youth. Genesis 22:1-10.

Then "the angel of the LORD *[YHWH]* called unto him out of heaven, and said: 'Abraham, Abraham.' And he said: 'Here am I.' And he said: 'Lay not thy hand upon the lad, neither do thou any thing unto him; for now I know that thou art a God-fearing man, seeing thou hast not withheld thy son, thine only *[yachid]* son, from Me.' " Verses 11, 12.

The identity of "the angel of the LORD" in this story was a subject of discussion among the rabbinical sages of early post-Biblical times. Their views concerning him differed considerably.

Note, first, that this celestial personage is said to be "the angel of the LORD," which seems to imply that he was not the LORD Himself, but was only His messenger.

However, that same "angel of the LORD," in deterring Abraham from slaying Isaac, commended the devotion and loyalty of the patriarch because "thou hast not withheld thy son . . . from Me." The use of the Word "Me" (capitalized) in that statement, implies that "the angel of the LORD" was the celestial personage who had commanded the patriarch to sacrifice the youth, and it was in loyal obedience to that same heavenly being that Abraham had not withheld his son.

Although this story about Abraham and Isaac is cited and discussed at least 13 times in the *Midrash Rabbah,* the *Midrash on Psalms,* and *Pesikta Rabbati,* the phrase "from Me" is omitted and apparently ignored in them. Why?

In the Greek version (LXX) the phrase "from Me" is rendered as "for my sake."[1] The Targum of Onkelos interprets it as "for Me;" and the Targum of Palestine as "from Me."

In specific reference to this story concerning Abraham and Isaac, it is said: "The single, definite, previously mentioned appearance of an Elohim is called 'ha-Elohim,' being as such synonymous with 'Mal'ak YHWH' (Gen. xxii. 3, 9, 11, 15), both speaking for YHWH (verse 16; comp. xlviii, 15)."[2] Note that here we have the angel of the LORD speaking in behalf of the LORD.

According to Genesis 22:1 the command to offer Isaac as a burnt-offering was given to Abraham by "God"—in Hebrew *ha-'Elohim,* which is a plural name with the definite article "the" *(ha)* prefixed. And in verses 8 and 12 the term *'Elohim* is used two more times. Was "the angel of the LORD" one of the *'Elohim?*

One Midrashic work simply identifies the messenger of the Lord as "an angel from heaven."[3] Another interprets Genesis 22:11, 12 to mean that to Abraham "God said: 'Now I know that thou art a God-fearing man' (Gen. 12:12)."[4]

Another has identified that same celestial being as the Deity in this manner: "Now the Holy One, blessed be He, said: 'This Abraham is God-fearing,' as it says, *Now I know that thou art a God-fearing man* (Gen. xxii, 12);" etc.[5] Still another writer identifies the heavenly messenger in this manner: "Then the Holy One, blessed be He, said to him: *'Lay not thy hand upon the lad'* (ib. 12)."[6]

Yet another rabbinical writer says that Abraham "took the knife in his hand to slay him. Indeed, had not the Holy One said to Abraham *Lay not thy hand upon the lad* (Gen. 22:12), Isaac would have been slain."[7]

Both of those statements seem to identify the "angel of the Lord" as "the Holy One," an expression often used in reference to the Deity.

That view was not a new one among the Jewish teachers of long ago. Philo Judaeus (born *c.* 20 B.C.E.; died after 40 C.E.) wrote that Abraham "having taken his knife in his right hand, he raised it over him [Isaac] as if to slay him; but God our Saviour stopped the deed in the middle, interrupting him by a voice from heaven, by which He ordered him to stay his hand, and not to touch the child: calling the father by name twice, so as to turn him and divert him from his purpose, and forbid him to complete [or, end] the sacrifice."[8]

"A Second Time"

After relating that the patriarch offered the ram for a sacrifice instead of Isaac, the Biblical narrative goes on to say: "The angel of the LORD [YHWH] called unto Abraham a second time out of heaven, and said: 'By Myself have I sworn, saith the LORD [YHWH], because thou hast done this thing, and hast not withheld thy son, thine only son, that in blessing I will bless thee," etc. Genesis 22:15, 16.

That makes it quite clear that the messenger of the LORD (YHWH) was now bearing a message from Him. He indicates this by the pharse, "saith the LORD [YHWH]," This and the phrase "from Me" in verse 12 imply that the heavenly messenger Himself in this experience of Abraham was not one of the common angels who serve the Deity. His relationship to, and association with, the Godhead, insofar as our world is concerned, are much closer and higher than many of us are aware of. Could he be Michael—the "One Who Is Like God"—and as such a person be one of the 'Elohim mentioned in verses 1, 3, 8, 9, 12?

One ancient rabbinical work comments: "At once the [Word of] the Holy One, blessed be He, leaped out to him: *By Myself have I sworn, saith the Lord, because,* etc., etc., *thy son, thine only one* (Gen. 22:16)."[9]

"In Abraham's case it is written, *'And the* angel *of the Lord called unto Abraham'* [Gen. XXII, 15], i.e. the angel it was that 'called' and the divine word that 'spoke,' " etc.[10]

A well known Jewish reference work aptly remarks: "In the

39

earlier Biblical writings the term *'Malak YHWH'* (messenger of the Lord), occurs chiefly in the singular, and signifies a special self-manifestation of God.'"[11]

Michael

Elsewhere it is said: "The Lord sent Michael the archangel to tell Abraham not to sacrifice his son."[12] Again: "Michael prevented Isaac from being sacrificed by his father by substituting a ram in his place ("Yalk. Reubeni," sect. 'Wayera.')"[13]

That view concerning the "angel of the Lord" (in Genesis 22) as Michael and "a self-manifestation of God" is a very interesting and thought-provoking one. It is worthy of our careful and prayerful consideration. It is not a new doctrine, but one that has come down from Israel's religious teachers of long, long ago through the ages.

One ancient rabbinical work gives this explanation: "Thereupon the Holy One, blessed be He, said to Michael: 'Why dost thou stand still? Do not let Abraham go on!' Michael began calling Abraham: *The angel of the Lord called unto him out of heaven, and said: 'Abraham, Abraham'* (Gen. 22:11), in rapid succession. For Abraham was hastening to cut Isaac's throat, and like a man crying out in sharp distress, the angel burst out at him: 'What art thou at?' Abraham turned his face toward the angel. When the angel burst out: 'What art thou at? *Lay not thy hand upon the lad!'* (Gen. 22:12), Abraham asked: Then shall I strangle him? The angel replied: *Neither do thou anything unto him! (ibid).* Abraham said: The plain fact is that the Holy One, blessed be He, Himself, told me to offer up my son, and yet thou sayest, 'Do not offer him up?' "[14]

Continued Guidance

The patriarchal story concerning Michael, Israel's Angel extraordinary, did not end with the intervention to save Isaac from death by the hand of his father Abraham on Mount Moriah. That wonderful archangel had a part later in the search for a suitable wife for Isaac, who would by her become the father of

Jacob and Esau.

When Isaac was 40 years old his father, now 140 years of age, saw that he needed a wife, and that the choice of a Canaanite woman to be his son's life companion would be unwise. The result of the marriage of Lot, Abraham's nephew and kinsman of Isaac, had demonstrated the results of intermarriage between a God-fearing man and a heathen woman. Therefore, Abraham sent his eldest and most trusted servant Eliezer of Damascus to Haran in Mesopotamia to find among the patriarch's relatives a suitable wife for Isaac. In sending his servant on that mission, Abraham, who was a prophet (Genesis 20:7), gave him this assurance: "The Lord, . . . will send His angel before thee." Genesis 24:7, 40.

The trusted servant's mission was successful, as narrated in Genesis 24.

In Jewish belief today that angel was Michael. Concerning Abraham's assurance to Eliezer that God would send His angel before him, "R. Dosa said: A particular angel is meant."[15] The editorial footnote comments: "Rashash: *malak* in the Heb. does not mean messenger, as often, but actually an angel. Mah.: Michael."[16]

What a wonderful demonstration of God's love for sinful humanity that He would send Michael, the celestial being highest in rank next to Him, to guide and protect Abraham's servant in this important mission! In a certain sense it was done for all of us, for it was God's purpose that in Abraham and his seed all the families—yes, all the nations—of the earth should be richly blessed.[17]

We need to study and understand better the role of Michael, the archangel, in God's plan for Israel and the rest of mankind.

FOOTNOTES AND REFERENCES

1. Genesis 22:12, Septuagint (LXX).
2. *The Jewish Encyclopedia,* vol. 5, page 604, col. 1.
3. *Midrash Rabbah* on Ecclesiastes, chap. 9, sect. 7, part 1 (page 232).
4. *The Midrash on Psalms,* Psalm 25, sect. 12 (vol. 1, page 354).
5. *Midrash Rabbah* on Genesis, chap. 49, sect. 2 (vol. 1, page 421).

6. *Ibid.* on Numbers, chap. 17, sect. 2 (vol. 2, pages 699, 700). In this the celestial speaker in Genesis 22:1, 2 is referred to as "the Holy One."

7. *Pesikta de-Rab Kahana,* piska 26, page 398.

8. Philo Judaeus, *On Abraham,* chap. 32 (vol. 2, page 432).

9. *Pesikta Rabbati,* piska 40, sect. 6 (vol. 2, page 719). *Note:* The bracketed matter—[Word of]—appears in the published English text, and has not been supplied by someone else. In the *Pesikta Rabbati,* piska 3, sects. 3 and 4; piska 5, sect. 11; "the Divine Word" is said to have played a role in God's dealings with the patriarch. A precedent for this was found in the frequent mention of "the Word" as an associate of the Lord in His dealings with men.

10. *Midrash Rabbah* on Leviticus, chap. 1, sect. 9 (page 13).

11. *The Jewish Encyclopedia,* vol. 1, page 589, col. 1.

12. *Ibid.,* page 87, col. 1.

13. *Ibid.,* vol. 8, page 536, col. 1.

14. *Pesikta Rabbati,* piska 40, sect. 6 (vol. 2, pages 718, 719).

15. *Midrash Rabbah* on Genesis, chap. 59, sect. 10 (vol. 2, page 522).

16. *Ibid.,* Footnote no. 5.

17. Genesis 12:3; 18:18; 22:18; 26:4; 28:14.

Chapter 5

MICHAEL AND JACOB

IT WAS not until 20 years after his marriage to Rebekah that Isaac's twin sons, Esau and Jacob, were born. Isaac was then 60 years old, and Abraham had reached the age of 160. When the twins were about 70 years old their feelings toward each other became so strained that Jacob fled to his Uncle Laban, his mother's brother, in Haran, in order to escape death at the hand of Esau.

At Bethel

Jacob spent the first night of his flight at a place called Luz, and lay down on the ground there with a stone for his pillow. The weary fugitive was given a wonderful dream during the night. "He dreamed, and behold a ladder set up on the earth, and the top of it reached to heaven; and behold the angels of God ascending and descending on it. And, behold, the LORD [YHWH] stood beside him, and said: 'I am the LORD [YHWH], the God of Abraham thy father, and the God of Isaac. The land whereon thou liest, to thee will I give it, and to thy seed. And thy seed shall be as the dust of the earth, and thou shalt spread abroad to the west, and to the east, and to the north, and to the south. And in thee and in thy seed shall all the families of the earth be blessed." Genesis 28:12-14.

When Jacob awoke he was so impressed by the dream that he said: " 'Surely the LORD [YHWH] is in this place; and I knew it not.' . . . 'This is none other than the house of God, and this is the gate of heaven.' " Verses 16, 17.

As the result, he called that place Bethel, which means "House of God." Verse 19. In fact, he marked the spot by setting up there as a pillar the stone which he had used as a pillow, and anointed it with oil. This place called Bethel became a religious landmark in the history of Palestine.

Years later, while in Egypt, the aged Jacob recalled those experiences saying: *"God Almightly appeared unto me at Luz in the land of Canaan, and blessed me."* Genesis 48:3. Luz was another name for Bethel. Genesis 28:19.

How assuring and comforting the promises which God gave to him that night at Bethel must have been to Jacob then and during the rest of his troubled life! According to the Mosaic account, the Lord said to Jacob: "Behold, I am with thee, and will keep thee whithersoever thou goest, and will bring thee back into this land; for I will not leave thee, until I have done that which I have spoken to thee of." Verse 15. Jacob accepted that promise with heartfelt gratitude.

In the course of time the rabbincial exegetes used the term "Memra" as a substitute for "the LORD" (YHWH) in speaking of God. They deemed it more reverent to speak of Him as the *Memra* ("Word"), the Greek equivalent of which was *Logos*. In this sense we are told concerning the term *"Memra"*: "It is the guardian of Jacob (Gen. xxviii. 20-21, xxxv. 3) and of Israel (Targ. Yer. to Ex. xii. 23, 29);" etc.[1] Where the Lord says in Genesis 28:15 "I am with thee," the Targums have him saying, "My Word shall be thy help," and "My Word is for thy help."

One thing that stands out prominently in the rabbinical discussion of Genesis 28 is the fact that some of the rabbis identified "the LORD" with Michael or *Memra* (the Word).

At Haran

Jacob finally arrived at Haran, where the relatives of Abraham and Sarah had lived. There he worked for his uncle Laban, married two of his daughters, and became the father of eleven sons and one daughter. Because of the prosperity enjoyed by Jacob under the blessing of God during his 20 years of employment by Laban, Jacob became the victim of envy and jealousy on the part of Laban's sons. Distressed by all this, Jacob was greatly perplexed, and wondered what he should do next. It was in this time of dire need that "the LORD said to Jacob: 'Return unto the land of thy fathers, and to thy kindred; and I will be with thee.' '' Genesis 31:3.

When Jacob talked with his family about this distressing situation he said: "The angel of God said unto me in the dream: . . . I am the God of Bethel, where thou didst anoint a pillar," etc. Verses 11, 13. Note that this angel said, "I am the God of Bethel." That makes it unmistakably clear and emphatic that "the angel of the Lord" speaking to Jacob in chapters 28 and 31 of Genesis was a being far superior to an ordinary angel. It is for this reason that we refer to him as Israel's Angel extraordinary.

One targumist of long ago interpreted Genesis 31:3 to mean this: "And the Lord said to Jacob, Return to thy country and to thy native (place): and My Word shall be for thy help."[2] Another targumist interprets it in a similar manner.[3]

Again, verse 13 is interpreted by a targumist in this manner: "The angel of the Lord said to me in a dream, Jacob. And I said, Behold, I am. And he said, . . . I am Eloha [the God] who appeared to thee at Bethel, where thou didst anoint the pillar."[4] Another targumist gives that verse the same interpretation.[5]

One of Judaism's most widely used reference works has rightly commented: "In the earlier Biblical writings the term 'malak *YHWH*, (messenger of the Lord) occurs chiefly in the singular and signifies a special self-manifestation of God (see Gen. xxxi, 11-13), where the angel of God says, 'I am the God of Bethel;' '' etc.[6]

Michael Interposed

Jacob and his family, in obedience to the Lord's directive (Genesis 31:3), quickly departed to go back to Canaan, the land of his birth, while Laban and his sons were elsewhere shearing sheep. Jacob was then about 96 years old.

When Laban was informed three days later that Jacob and his family had fled, he and a band of men pursued him and overtook them near Mt. Gilead about a week later. "And God came

45

to Laban the Aramean in a dream of the night, and said unto him: 'Take heed to thyself that thou speak not to Jacob either good or bad.' " Verses 22-25.

Which one of the *Elohim* ("God") in verse 24 warned Laban against doing harm to Jacob? A modern Jewish opinion on that point reads: "Michael prevented Laban from harming Jacob (Pirke R. El. xxxvi.)"[7]

An ancient rabbinical work attributed to R. Eliezer b. Hyrcanus,[8] a noted tanna of the first and second centuries C.E., says: "And Laban took all the men of his city, mighty men, and he pursued after him [Jacob], seeking to slay him. The angel Michael descended, and drew his sword behind him, seeking to slay him. He said to him: Do not speak to Jacob, either good or bad, as it is said, 'And God came to Laban the Aramean in a dream of the night, and said unto him, Take heed to thyself that thou speak not to Jacob either good or bad.'"[9]

After they made a covenant of peace between them, Laban and his men returned to Haran and Jacob and his household proceeded toward Canaan. Genesis 31:48-54; 32:1.

At Mahanaim

When Jacob and his family arrived at Mahanaim, near the river Jabbok, they encamped there. He then became aware of the fact that he was in danger of being attacked by his brother Esau, who was coming to meet him with a band of 400 men.[10] Thus threatened, Jacob sent messengers and abundant presents, with a message of appeasement, to his brother Esau. After the members of his family had crossed the Jabbok at the ford and encamped there, Jacob went apart to spend the night in earnest prayer to God for His favor and protection.

While he was praying, Jacob was suddenly seized in the darkness by a strong hand. Fearing an assailant was bent on killing him, Jacob wrestled with the stranger until daybreak. Here is the story as it is told in Holy Writ:

"There wrestled a man with him [Jacob] until the breaking of the day. And when he saw that he prevailed not against him,

46

he touched the hollow of his thigh; and the hollow of Jacob's thigh was strained, as he wrestled with him. And he said: 'Let me go, for the day breaketh.' And he said: 'I will not let thee go, except thou bless me.' And he said unto him: 'What is thy name?' And he said: 'Jacob.' And he said: 'Thy name shall be called no more Jacob, but Israel; for thou hast striven with God and with men, and hast prevailed. And Jacob asked him, and said: 'Tell me, I pray thee, thy name.' And he said: 'Wherefore is it that thou dost ask after my name?' And he blessed him there. And Jacob called the name of the place Peniel: 'for I have seen God face to face, and my life is preserved.' " Genesis 32:25-31.

It must have been a tremendous surprise for Jacob when his antagonist revealed his identity to him!

Who Wrestled With Jacob?

Who was the person that wrestled with Jacob that night? Verse 25 refers to him as "a man." The Targum of Palestine to this passage says that he was an "angel . . . in the guise of a man."

That he was a holy angel in the guise of a man is evident from Jacob's later reference to him as "the angel who hath redeemed me from all evil." Genesis 48:16.

Centuries later a prophet said that "he [Jacob] strove with an angel" (*mal'ak*, in Hebrew). Hosea 12:5, Hebrew text.

Michael

The heavenly being with whom Jacob strove was not an ordinary angel *(mal'ak)*. It is believed that he was Israel's Angel extraordinary, the celestial being called Michael in the Holy Scriptures. His name, as we have shown previously in this book, means "Who Is Like God."

A modern Jewish reference work says concerning Michael: "He is identified with the angel who wrestled with Jacob and later blessed him."[11]

Another such work tells us that, while some held contrary opinions, "others identify him with the angel Michael."[12]

And one rabbinical tradition says that "the angel Samael [Satan] was about to kill Jacob, when Michael intervened."[13]

Elsewhere the same work informs its readers: "It was Michael, too, who wrestled with Jacob and who afterward blessed him (Targ. pseudo-Jonathan to Gen. xxxii. 25; Pirke R. El. xxxvii.)."[14]

In reference to the angel's statement to Jacob, "Let me go, for the day breaketh" (Genesis 32:27), a Midrashic work says: "It was Michael or Gabriel, who are celestial princes."[15]

Another Midrashic statement sets forth the same idea: "The angels [concerned in the incident with Jacob] were Gabriel and Michael] who were celestial princes."[16]

When it was almost dawn the angel who wrestled with Jacob said: "Let me go, for the day breaketh." Verse 27. In obvious reference to this, the Targum of Palestine says concerning Michael that he "remained from God at the torrent [of Jabbok] till the column of the morning was ascending." Did the writer of that statement mean to say that Michael had come from God to Jacob, or been sent by Him to the patriarch?

The Angel Extraordinary

The celestial being who wrestled with Jacob was one whom we may regard as extraordinary. We need to note carefully what the Mosaic record says concerning him.

First, when he bestowed upon Jacob the name "Israel," the heavenly messenger said: "Thy name shall be called no more Jacob, but Israel; for *thou has striven with God*." Verse 29. The last syllable in that new name is "el" (*'El* in Hebrew), which means "God." The reason given for its bestowal on the patriarch is explained by the heavenly being himself, saying: "Thou hast striven with God" [*'Elohim* in the Hebrew text]. Thus the celestial being with whom Jacob wrestled definitely identifies himself with the Holy One.

Second, as a result of this remarkable experience Jacob gave to the place at which it occurred the name "Peniel," that is, "The face of God."[17] The last syllable of the name "Peniel" is *el,* which means "God" in Hebrew.

Third, Jacob explained why he gave the name "Peniel" to that place, saying: "I have seen God *['Elohim]* face to face." Verse 31.[18]

Fourth, later, in blessing Joseph and his two sons, Jacob specifically identified that extraordinary angel *(mal'ak)* as the Holy One of Israel by saying: "The God before whom my fathers Abraham and Isaac did walk, the God who hath been my shepherd all my life long unto this day, the angel who hath redeemed me from all evil, bless the lads." Genesis 48:15, 16.

Fifth, Centuries later, one of Israel's prophets referred to that experience of Jacob by saying, according to the Hebrew text, that "he contended with God *['Elohim].* Yes, he contended with the Angel *[mal'ak]* and prevailed." Hosea 12:4, 5. A widely used Jewish reference work of modern times aptly remarks: "Hosea alludes to Jacob's wrestling with the angel, whom he calls once 'Elohim' and once 'Mal'ak.' "[19]

It is amazing and even shocking to see that some of Israel's teachers have presumed to modify or alter what God's prophet has so clearly said to His people. For example, one translation renders into English the term *'Elohim* in Hosea 12:4 as "a godlike being."[20] Isaac Leeser renders it as "an angel." Alexander Harkavy correctly renders it as "God."

In translating Genesis 32:29, the Hebrew term *'Elohim* has been correctly rendered as "God" by Isaac Leeser and Alexander Harkavy, and by the translators of the text published by the Jewish Publication Society in 1917; but as "beings divine" in the English text entitled *Torah,* published in 1962. The aversion is not new, for the Targum of Palestine to Genesis 32:29 says: "Thou art magnified with the angels of the Lord and with the mighty." The Targum of Onkelos interprets it to mean "a prince art thou before the Lord." The *Midrash Rabbah* to Genesis has left the term *'Elohim* uninterpreted in quoting this verse.[21]

We must not presume to alter the Sacred Scriptures to make them conform to human opinions that contradict it. And we dare not assume that Moses and the other prophets of the God of

Israel penned falsehoods for His people and the rest of mankind to believe during the centuries thereafter.

The Holy Scriptures clearly show that the celestial messenger *(mal'ak)* who appeared to the patriarch Jacob was not an ordinary angel. We may reasonably deem him to be Michael, Israel's Angel extraordinary, whose name means "Who Is Like God," as many of Israel's teachers of long ago have taught.

FOOTNOTES AND REFERENCES

1. *The Jewish Encyclopedia,* vol. 8, page 465, col. 1.
2. *Targum of Onkelos,* vol. 1, page 103.
3. *Targum of Palestine,* vol. 1, page 264.
4. *Targum of Onkelos,* chap. 7, sect. 31, vol. 1, page 104.
5. *Targum of Palestine,* chap. 7, sect. 31, vol. 1, pages 264, 265.
6. *The Jewish Encyclopedia,* vol. 1, page 589, col. 1.
7. *Ibid.,* vol. 8, page 536, col. 1.
8. See *Ibid,* vol. 5, page 115, col. 1, art.; "Eliezer b. Hyrcanus;" vol. 10, page 58, col. 1, art., "Pirke de-Rabbi Eli'ezer."
9. *Pirke de Rabbi Eliezer,* chap. 36, page 273.
10. Genesis 32:1-7.
11. *The Universal Jewish Encyclopedia,* vol. 7, page 529, col. 2.
12. *The Jewish Encyclopedia,* vol. 7, page 23, col. 1.
13. *Ibid.,* page 22, col. 1.
14. *Ibid.,* vol. 8, page 536, col. 1. The Targum here referred to is the one better known as the Targum of Palestine. See J. W. Etheridge, Targum of Palestine on Genesis, vol. 1, page 157.
15. *Midrash Rabbah* on Genesis, chap. 78, sect. 1 (vol. 2, page 714).
16. *Ibid.,* on Lamentations, chap. 3, sect. 8 (page 201).
17. See the footnote to Genesis 32:21 in the JPS version.
18. See *The Jewish Encyclopedia,* vol. 7, page 21, col. 1.
19. *Ibid.*
20. The Jewish Publication Society version of 1917.
21. *Midrash Rabbah* on Genesis, chap. 78, sect. 3 (vol. 2, page 717).

Chapter 6

MICHAEL AND MOSES

MOSES, at the time of Israel's exodus from Egypt, had been for 40 years on the Egyptian FBI's list of most wanted men. Though born the second son of enslaved Hebrew parents near the River Nile, he was by divine providence adopted by a princess of Egypt's reigning Pharaoh. Although he had been given the education and training of an Egyptian prince, and was a candidate for kingly honors in the future, he never ceased to be at heart a Hebrew and a devout believer in the God of Israel.

A sudden turn in the life of Moses came when, at the age of approximately 40 years, he saw an Egyptian taskmaster cruelly beating a Hebrew slave. Instantly Moses slew the taskmaster and buried him in the sand. Sensing the fact that he had committed a serious crime in the eyes of the Egyptians, he fled to Midian, the land occupied by the descendants of Abraham and his second wife, Keturah. There he married Zipporah, the daughter of Jethro, the priest and prince of Midian, who was a worshiper of the true God.

When he was 80 years old, Moses experienced another sudden turn in his life while herding his father-in-law's flocks in the wilderness near Mt. Horeb, which is also called Mount Sinai. Little did he then imagine what the next 40 years of his life in that region would be. Here is the way that third 40-year period of his life began:

"And the angel of the LORD [YHWH] appeared unto him in a flame of fire out of the midst of a bush; and he looked, and, behold the bush burned with fire, and the bush was not consumed. And Moses said: 'I will turn aside now, and see this great sight, why the bush is not burnt.' And when the LORD [YHWH] saw that he turned aside to see, God called unto him out of the midst of the bush, and said: 'Moses, Moses.' And he said: 'Here am I.' And He said: 'Draw not nigh hither; put off thy shoes from off thy feet, for the place whereon thou standest is holy ground.' Moreover, He said: 'I am the God of thy father, the God of Abraham, the God of Isaac, and the God of Jacob.' And Moses hid his face; for he was afraid to look upon God. And the Lord said: 'I have surely seen the affliction of My people that are in Egypt, and have heard their cry by reason of their taskmasters; for I know their pains.' '' Exodus 3:2-7.

At that time the LORD (YHWH) commissioned Moses to bear for Him a message to Pharaoh king of Egypt to let the enslaved Hebrew people leave that country to go to the land of Canaan.

A Remarkable Angel

One Jewish reference work has made this interesting and thought-provoking statement concerning that angel *(mal'ak)* which spoke to Moses from the burning bush: ''In the earlier Biblical writings the term 'Malak YHWH' (messenger of the Lord) occurs chiefly in the singular, and signifies a special self-manifestation of God (see Gen. xxxi. 11-13, where the angel of God says, 'I am the God of Bethel'; Ex. iii. 2-6, where the angel of the Lord who appeared to Moses in the flame of fire says, 'I am the God of thy father'; compare Gen. xxii. 11; Judges, vi. 11-22).''[1]

The fact of the deity of Israel's Angel extraordinary in this case is recorded in the Holy Scriptures by Moses himself. Of special interest is the role that He, the heavenly messenger *(malak),* played in Israel's deliverance from Egyptian bondage.

As we consider it, we must keep in mind that this was an experience in which Moses himself was personally involved and not one which had happened long before he lived. A modern Jewish writer has aptly stated that fact in the following words: ''As he is feeding the sheep on Mount Horeb, he has a marvelous experience. God appears to him from a thorn-bush which, though burning, is not consumed. He reveals Himself as the God of the Fathers of Israel, and orders Moses to go before Pharaoh and demand the release of his brethren."[2]

The Lord then told Moses to return to Egypt and lead the people of Israel out to Canaan, the land which God had promised to Abraham and his seed 400 years before.[3] Startled by this sudden and tremendous commission, "Moses said unto God: 'Behold, when I come unto the children of Israel, and shall say unto them: The God of your fathers hath sent me unto you; and they shall say to me: What is His name? what shall I say unto them? And God said unto Moses: 'I AM THAT I AM'; and He said: 'Thus shalt thou say unto the children of Israel: I AM hath sent me unto you.' And God said moreover unto Moses: 'Thus shalt thou say unto the children of Israel: The LORD [YHWH], the God of your fathers, the God of Abraham, the God of Isaac, and the God of Jacob, hath sent me unto you.' " Exodus 3:13-15.

The deity of the celestial being who spoke to Moses on this occasion is so unmistakably obvious that in this translation of the Hebrew text into English by able Jewish Biblical scholars, and published for many years for the people to read, the words "he" and "my" are capitalized—as "He" and "My"—when used in reference to Him in this narrative penned by Moses under divine inspiration.

Shortly before his death 40 years later, Moses invoked the blessing of the LORD (YHWH) upon the tribes of Israel, and especially upon that of Joseph "the good will of Him that dwelt in the bush." Deuteronomy 33:16.

We are told: "When he [Moses] turned aside to look more closely at the marvel, YHWH spoke to him from the bush and commissioned him to return to Egypt and deliver his brethren from their bondage (Ex. iii. 1-10). According to Ex. iii. 13 *et. seq.,* it was at this time that the name of YHWH was revealed, though it is frequently used throughout the patriarchal narratives, from the second chapter of Genesis on."[4]

The Exodus

Not until the Lord had broken Pharaoh's defiant spirit and reduced Egypt to ruins and to mourning by 10 terrible plagues, was Israel given royal permission to leave Egypt. The exodus of the liberated people from the land of their bondage began at midnight of Abib (Nisan) 14, and by morning the Israelite host—men, women, children, wagons, herds, flocks, and their possessions—were on their way.

When the vast hosts of Israel—approximately two and a half million people—marched out of Egypt, "the LORD [YHWH] went before them by day in a pillar of cloud, to lead them the way; and by night in a pillar of fire, to give them light; that they might go by day and by night: the pillar of cloud by day, and the pillar of fire by night, departed not from before the people." Exodus 13:21, 22.

Such was the love, care, and protection of Israel's Angel extraordinary for His people in that great crisis.

At the Sea

Soon after they left Egypt the Lord directed Moses to have Israel encamp beside Pi-hahiroth by the sea. Exodus 14:2,9. When Pharaoh heard of this, he hastily led a military force consisting of more than 600 chariots, in pursuit of the Israelites, hoping to overtake them. The Egyptian king and his army cornered the Israelites at a strategic place by the sea at night.

Then "the angel of God, who went before the camp of Israel, removed and went behind them; and the pillar of cloud removed from before them, and stood behind them; and it came between the camp of Egypt and the camp of Israel; and there was the cloud and the darkness here, yet gave it light by night there; and the one came not near the other all the night." Exodus 14:19, 20.

Note particularly that "the angel of God" in the pillar of cloud was watching over and protecting Israel from both the front and the rear.

The Word

"And it came to pass in the morning watch, that the LORD [YHWH] looked forth upon the host of the Egyptians through the pillar of fire and of cloud, and discomfited the host of the Egyptians." Verse 24.

The Targum of Jerusalem to Exodus 13:18 states that "the Word of the Lord conducted the people by the way of the desert of the sea of Suph." And in Exodus 14:24 it says that "the Word of the Lord looked upon the host of Mizraee [Egyptians], . . and conturbed the host of the Mizraee."[5]

Nearly 40 years later Moses reminded Israel of their anguish as slaves in Egypt, saying: "When we cried unto the LORD, He heard our voice, and sent an angel, and brought us forth out of Egypt." Numbers 20:16. See also Numbers 14:14.

One rabbinical work says concerning that experience at the Red Sea: "Moses spake before the Holy One, blessed be He, saying: Sovereign of all worlds! The enemy is behind them, and the sea is in front of them, which way shall they go forward? What did the Holy One, blessed be He, do? He sent Michael, and he became a wall of fire between (Israel and) the Egyptians."[6]

FOOTNOTES AND REFERENCES

1. *The Jewish Encyclopedia,* vol. 1, page 589, col. 1.
2. *Ibid.,* vol. 5, page 297, col. 1.
3. Genesis 15:13-20.
4. *The Jewish Encyclopedia,* vol. 9, page 44, col. 2.
5. *Targum of Jerusalem,* Etheridge, vol. 2, pages 484 and 490.
6. *Pirke de Rabbi Eliezer,* chap. 42, page 329.

Chapter 7

MICHAEL AT SINAI

Approximately six weeks (Exodus 19:1) after they left Egypt, the vast host of liberated Israelites encamped at Mount Sinai. A modern writer has well described it in this graphic manner:

"From Rephidim, the people continued their journey, following the movement of the cloudy pillar. Their route had led across barren plains, over steep ascents, and through rocky defiles. Often as they had traversed the sandy wastes, they had seen before them rugged mountains, like huge bulwarks, piled up directly across their course, and seeming to forbid all further progress. But as they approached, openings here and there appeared in the mountain wall, and beyond, another plain opened to view. Through one of these deep, gravelly passes they were now led. It was a grand and impressive scene. Between the rocky cliffs rising hundreds of feet on either side, flowed in a living tide, as far as the eye could reach, the hosts of Israel with their flocks and herds. And now before them in solemn majesty Mount Sinai lifted its massive front. The cloudy pillar rested upon its summit, and the people spread their tents upon the plain beneath. Here was to be their home for nearly a year. At night the pillar of fire assured them of the divine protection, and while they were locked in slumber, the bread of heaven fell gently upon the encampment.

"The dawn gilded the dark ridges of the mountains, and the sun's golden rays pierced the deep gorges, seeming to those weary travelers like beams of mercy from the throne of God. On every hand, vast, rugged heights seemed in their solitary grandeur to speak of eternal endurance and majesty. Here the mind was impressed with solemnity and awe. Man was made to feel his ignorance and weakness in the presence of Him who 'weighed the mountains in scales, and the hills in a balance' (Isa. 40:12). Here

Israel was to receive the most wonderful revelation ever made by God to men. Here the Lord had gathered His people that He might impress upon them the sacredness of His requirements by declaring with His own voice His holy law.

"Great and radical changes were to be wrought in them; for the degrading influences of servitude and a long-continued association with idolatry had left their mark upon habits and character. God was working to lift them to a higher moral level by giving them a knowledge of Himself."[1]

The Theocracy Established

At that time the Lord took Israel, as a nation, into a special covenant relationship with Himself in order to fulfill His plan for them to be a blessing to the whole world, as He had foretold centuries before.[2] He said to Israel:

"If ye will hearken unto My voice indeed, and keep My covenant, then ye shall be Mine own treasure from among all peoples; for all the earth is Mine; and ye shall be unto Me a kingdom of priests, and a holy nation." Exodus 19:5,6. "And all the people answered together, and said: 'All that the LORD hath spoken we will do.' " Verse 8.

Immediately thereafter the Lord spoke in awful grandeur and majesty the Ten Commandments from the summit of Mount Sinai. Exodus 20:1-14. Also He gave to Moses some basic statutes essential to the government of the nation.[3]

Shortly thereafter that covenant solemnly made between God and Israel as a nation was formally ratified. Exodus 24. Thereby Israel became a theocracy under God as their Ruler, Lawgiver, and Judge.

The Myriads

God was not alone when He spoke the Ten Commandments from the summit of Mount Sinai. Nearly 40 years later Moses reminded Israel of that fact: "The Lord came from Sinai, and rose up from Seir unto them; He shined forth from mount Paran, and He came from the myriads holy, at His right hand was a fiery law unto them." Deuteronomy 33:2.

Many readers are puzzled by the phrase "the myriads holy" in that verse. The Hebrew text actually says: "and came from among myriads a Holy One." The Hebrew word rendered as "Holy One" is the noun *qadosh*, and is singular in number and not plural. The question now is this: Who were "the myriads"?

In specific reference to this particular experience recorded by Moses the ancient rabbis spoke of them as "a vast number of angels." For instance, the Targum of Onkelos to Deuteronomy 33:2 says that they were "ten thousand saints." The Targum of Palestine interprets it to mean that there were with them "ten thousand times ten thousand holy angels."

That interpretation is not correct because the Hebrew noun *qadosh* is not a plural adjective modifying the noun rendered as "myriads."

One rabbinical work of long ago enthusiastically declared them to be "sixty myriads of ministering angels," but R. Abba bar R. Kahana said: "One hundred and twenty myriads of ministering angels came down with the Holy One, blessed be He."[4]

In recounting this later to the king of Edom, Moses said: "When we cried unto the Lord, He heard our voice, and sent an angel, and brought us forth out of Egypt." Numbers 20:16. Thus the Angel called "LORD" [YHWH] was a celestial being distinct from the LORD [YHWH] who sent Him to defend and guide Israel.

"When Israel was marching through the wilderness, YHWH, wrapped in a pillar of cloud, preceded the people in order to show them the right way."[5]

During the centuries that Angel has been a subject of much thought among Jewish scholars. Says one source of information: "Michael led the Israelites during their forty years' wandering in the wilderness (Abravanel to Ex. xxiii. 20)."[6]

It is interesting to note, too, that in the major Messianic movement that began in the land of Israel in the first century C.E., it was taught that holy angels were present when God gave the laws to His people at Mount Sinai.[7]

Michael

Next for our consideration is this question: Who was the "Holy One" referred to by Moses as "*qadosh*," "a Holy One" in Deuteronomy 33:2?

An interesting Midrashic statement of long ago tells us that "when God came down on Sinai, there also came down with Him many companies of angels, Michael and his company, Gabriel and his company."[8]

A Jewish reference work calls its reader's attention to that Midrashic statement by saying: "Michael and Gabriel were . . . both among the angels who accompanied God when He came down on Mount Sinai (Deut. R. 2:34)."[9]

Michael, whose name signifies "Who Is Like God" is the one to whom we have referred in this book as "Israel's Angel extraordinary."

Michael was exceedingly popular among the people of Israel in ancient times. In Exodus 20:15-17 it is said that the people of Israel were filled with great awe and dread as they witnessed and listened while God was speaking from the summit of Mount Sinai. God in person was not visible to the people at that time for a great cloud veiled Him from their view, while there was a great manifestation of fire, smoke, thunder, and earth tremors which greatly frightened the people. After the giving of the Ten Commandments orally by God, "Moses drew near unto the thick darkness where God was." Verse 18. One Jewish writer has imagined it thus:

"The Holy One, blessed be He, heard the voice of Israel, and it was pleasing to Him, and He sent for Michael and Gabriel, and they took hold of the two hands of Moses against his will, and they brought him near unto the thick darkness."[10]

For many centuries the people of Israel have been taught to appreciate the role of Michael in God's plan for them. Here are a few examples of it:

"When He [God] gave the commandments on Mount Sinai, at first He uttered them loudly all at once, as is said, *And God spoke all these words [at once] saying* (Exod. 20:1). Thereupon

Michael said: He is about to commission me to explain His words."[11]

"But when He came down on Mount Sinai to give Torah to Israel, Michael and his retinue came down with Him," etc.[12]

"When the Holy One, blessed be He, came down on Mount Sinai, Michael and his retinue, Gabriel and his retinue, came down."[13] The editorial footnote to that passage says: "Michael, the Prince of Israel."[14]

Israel's Guiding Angel

Israel was encamped at Mount Sinai nearly a year. During that time the Lord was instructing His people and preparing them for their entrance into the Promised Land of Canaan and for the fulfillment of their religious mission to the rest of the world. Not only were they divinely equipped with the Holy Scriptures penned by Moses for use in their mission, but they were provided a sanctuary and an elaborate system of sacrificial offerings and religious feast days to serve as object lessons to aid them in their teaching of God's plan for the redemption of men.

Moreover, He supplied manna for food, water to drink, and instruction designed to preserve their health. Very precious was God's promise given to them soon after Israel was taken into a special covenant relationship with Him as "a kingdom of priests, and a holy nation" (Exodus 19:6).

"Behold, I send an angel before thee, to keep thee by the way, and to bring thee into the place which I have prepared. Take heed of him, and hearken unto his voice; be not rebellious against him; for he will not pardon your transgression; for My name is in him. But if thou shalt indeed hearken unto his voice, and do all that I speak; then I will be an enemy unto thine enemies, and an adversary unto thine adversaries. For Mine angel shall go before thee." Exodus 23:20-23.

Who was that promised angel guide? We are told that "Michael is credited also with having guided Israel safely through the wilderness."[15]

The fact that God calls him "Mine angel" implies that he has a special relationship to the Deity. The fact that He says "My name is in him," shows this to be the case. This is indicated in a very special way by his Hebrew name Michael, which literally means "Who Is Like God." He ranks so high in divine authority that Israel is admonished in the clearest of terms to accept his leadership and to faithfully follow his instructions. The people of Israel were solemnly warned individually and collectively not to disobey him. They were admonished to faithfully "take heed of him, and hearken unto his voice." To wilfully spurn and reject him would be an unpardonable sin, for God plainly warned them against that by saying: "Be not rebellious against him; for he will not pardon your transgression." Verse 21.

It is evident, then, that Michael is a very extraordinary celestial being very closely associated with the LORD [YHWH]. One Jewish concept is that "he is the medium for the transmission of the Law to Moses and Israel."[16]

He Spoke for God

Israel's Angel extraordinary was comissioned to speak for God to Israel, and His words were to be accepted as the will of our Creator. In comment on Exodus 23:22 this truth was emphatically stated in this Midrashic statement penned in the distant past: "It does not say 'that he speaks', but THAT I SPEAK, implying that if you receive his words it will be like listening to Me. If you will do this, THEN I WILL BE AN ENEMY UNTO THINE ENEMIES. Hence, BEHOLD, I SEND AN ANGEL."[17]

The promise that this Angel extraordinary would guide Israel into the Promised Land of Canaan, and that he would subdue their enemies before them, was repeated several times. See Exodus 32:34; 33:2. How tragic it was to Israel when the vast majority of the 12 spies, and the majority of the people, when they heard their report (Numbers 13 and 14), refused to go forward in faith. As a result of unbelief almost all of those who were twenty years old and older at the time of the exodus from Egypt perished in the wilderness of their wandering during the next 38 years![18]

FOOTNOTES AND REFERENCES

1. E. G. White, *Patriarchs and Prophets,* pages 301, 302.
2. Genesis 12:3; 18:18; 22:18; 26:4; 28:14.
3. Exodus 20:19-23; 21:22; 23:1-19.
4. *Pesikta Rabbati,* Piska 33, sect. 10 (vol. 2, page 648). According to *The Jewish Encyclopedia,* vol. 12, page 50, col. 4, R. Abba bar Kahana was a Palestinian amora.
5. *Ibid.,* vol. 4, page 123, col. 1.
6. *Ibid.,* vol. 8, page 536, col. 2.
7. Acts of the Apostles 7:38,53; Hebrews 2:2. Paul [Saul] of Tarsus, one of the most prominent leaders of the great messianic movement which began among the Jews of Palestine in the first century C.E., stated in one of his letters: "Moreover, brethren, I would not that ye should be ignorant, how that all our fathers were under the cloud, and all passed through the sea; and were all baptized unto Moses in the cloud and in the sea; and did all eat the same spiritual meat; and did all drink the same spiritual drink: for they drank of that spiritual Rock that followed them: and that Rock was Christ." 1 Corinthians 10:1-4.
8. *Midrash Rabbah* on Deuteronomy, chap. 2, sect. 34 (page 63).
9. *The Encyclopedia Judaica,* vol. 11, col. 1489.
10. *Pirke de R. Eliezer,* chap. 41, page 325.
11. *Pesikta Rabbati,* Piska 21, sect. 5 (vol. 1, page 420).
12. *Ibid.,* sect. 9 (vol. 1, page 430).
13. *Ibid.,* sect. 11 (vol. 1, page 432).
14. *Ibid.,* Footnote no. 60.
15. *The Universal Jewish Encyclopedia,* vol. 7, page, 529, col. 2.
16. *Ibid.*
17. *Midrash Rabbah* to Exodus, chap. 32. sect. 4 (page 409).
18. Numbers 26:64,65; 32:8-12.

Chapter 8

ISRAEL'S GUARDIAN ANGEL

FOR THE ratification of the covenant between God and His people Israel, Moses and the leaders of the nation were bidden to come up to Him on Mount Sinai for that purpose. The record of the invitation given him to do this began with these words:

"Unto Moses He said: 'Come up unto the LORD, thou, and Aaron, Nadab, and Abihu, and seventy of the elders of Israel; and worship ye afar off.' " Exodus 24:1.

Who told Moses and the other leaders to come up to the Lord? That is, who was the person mentioned as "He" in the phrase "He said"? It was a great privilege and honor for the ones invited. Who was "He" who extended the invitation to them?

The Targum of Palestine to Exodus 24 interprets that passage thus: "Michael, the Prince of Wisdom, said to Mosheh on the seventh day of the month, Come up before the Lord, thou Aharon, Nadab and Abihu, and seventy of the elders of Israel, and worship at a distance."

That interpretation was based on the belief that the invitation recorded in Exodus 24:1 was given to Moses and his associates by Michael, Israel's Angel extraordinary, who is the celestial messenger whom God calls "Mine angel." Exodus 23:23. It is said, for example:

"Metatron bears the Tetragrammaton; for Ex. xxiii. 21, says, 'My name is in him.' "[1]

The following passage from the Babylonian Talmud illustrates how a prejudiced religious teacher in the distant past attempted to refute that view: "R. Nahman said: He who is skilled in refuting the *Minim* as is R. Idith, let him do so; but not otherwise. Once a *Min* said to R. Idith: It is written, *And unto Moses He said, Come up to the Lord.* But surely it should have stated, Come up unto Me!—It was Metatron [who said that], he replied, whose name is similar to that of his Master, for it is written, *For My name is in him.* But if so, [he retorted,] we should worship him! The same passage, however,—replied R. Idith—says: *Be not rebellious against him,* i.e., exchange Me not for him. But if so, why is it stated: *He will not pardon your transgression?*"[2]

An editorial footnote says of Metatron: "Name of an Angel, probably derived from *metator,* guide. In Talmud and Midrash he is regarded notably as the defender of the rights of Israel (cf. Hag. 16a)."[3]

A scholarly Jewish reference work, in comment on this, says that "Targ. Yer. to Ex. xxiv. 1 has Michael instead of Metatron. . . . Targ. Yer. to Ex. xxiv. 1 substitutes the name of Michael for Metatron."[4]

In the above-mentioned case of R. Idith (sometimes spelled Idi or Idit) and a *Min* (a Jew whom he regarded as a heretic) we have an interesting discussion that took place after the middle of the second century C.E. The *Min* held the old traditional belief that the Angel of God's presence, mentioned in Exodus 23:20-23, was a divine being closely associated with the Supreme Ruler of the universe. He, Michael, the one "Who Is Like God," not only bore the name of the Deity but was also His spokesman to man, spoke in His name, exercised His authority, and specially loved, guided, and protected His people Israel when they were loyally obedient to God. The person referred to above as a *Min* cited to the rabbi what Moses had recorded in Exodus 23:20-23.

In his attempt to refute the *Min's* argument, R. Idith could not accuse him of misquoting the Holy Scriptures. But the *Min* pointed out that if the passage meant what it actually says, then Israel's Angel extraordinary—the Messenger of God's presence—should be worshiped too!

R. Idith then questioned the integrity of the record penned by Israel's great prophet Moses, alleging that Exodus 24:1 should have said, "Come up unto Me" instead of "Come up unto the LORD [YHWH]."

R. Idith then alleged that the command concerning the Angel of the divine presence, "Be not rebellious against him" (Exodus 23:21), should have said, "Exchange Me not for him," as if what is *actually* written there by Moses, if taken as it reads, means to put another God in the place of the one whom he and Israel served. However, Exodus 23:20-23 does not say such a thing as that. It simply calls for man's cooperation with the true God by hearkening and rendering obedience to Michael, the divinely appointed intermediary of highest rank, the one who implements God's plans for the salvation of sinful man.

Another Observation

Another comment on that experience of R. Idith and the *Min* is worth consideration. It says:

"An unbeliever said to R. Idit, 'Why is it said in Ex. xxiv. 1, "And he said unto Moses, Come up unto the Lord"'? It should say, "Come up unto me." The rabbi answered: 'God in this place is the Metatron, whose name is as the name of his Lord.' " The footnote to that statement reads: 'The current explanation of this passage is that, according to R. Idit, YHWH does not always mean God in person, but sometimes an angel."[5]

A Midrashic work of long ago remarks: "At Sinai, too, Moses stood aside; said He to him, *Come up unto the Lord.*"[6] It is worthy of note that in that Midrashic statement the pronoun "He" is spelled with a capital "H". This is true also where that verse is quoted in other Midrashic works.

We have noted in a previous chapter that God was not alone when He came to Mount Sinai in the time of Moses. He was accompanied by myriads of holy angels, and with them was Michael, the archangel.

Michael

Michael is referred to as "Israel's guardian angel,"[7] and as "your advocate."[8] It is said that Michael's place is at God's right hand.[9]

Michael is frequently referred to by several different names. One of them is *Memra* (Word) in Aramaic, the equivalent of which in Greek is *Logos,* which means "Word." It is said of Michael as such that he "goes before Israel in the wilderness."[10]

Metatron

Another name by which Michael is frequently mentioned is *Metatron,* which is said to be a term of Greek derivation. It appears to have come into Jewish use through the Babylonian Talmud, for it is not found in the Palestinian.

One explanation of the term Metatron is that it comes "from the Greek *metathronon,* 'after (or nearest) the divine throne,' " etc.[11]

A Talmudic tractate speaks of Metatron as of one who instructed Israel in days of old. The editorial footnote to that passage in Abodah Zarah explains: "Metatron is probably derived from *Metator,* meaning guide, precursor, he being regarded as the angel who went before the Israelites in the wilderness."[12]

Another interesting item concerning the high regard shown for Metatron is this one: "The Karaite Kirkisani read in his text of the Talmud an even more extreme version: 'This is Metatron, who is the lesser YHWH.' "[13]

Concerning the identity of Metatron we are told: "Metatron, a term for the highest angel, found only in ancient times in Haggadic and Cabalistic literature. He is occasionally identified with the 'prince of the presence,' with the archangel Michael."[14]

Our Great Prince

Through His great seer Daniel the Lord has declared Michael to be "the great prince, who standeth for the children of thy people." Daniel 12:1. His role in the history of Israel has been a wonderful one, and he deserves to be greatly appreciated and loved by us for all that he has done for the human race throughout the generations since sin brought our planet into revolt against its Creator.

FOOTNOTES AND REFERENCES

1. *The Jewish Encyclopedia,* vol. 8, page 519, col. 1.
2. BT *Sanhedrin* 38b (pages 245, 246).
3. *Ibid.,* page 245, footnote no. 11.
4. *The Jewish Encyclopedia,* vol. 8, page 519, cols. 1,2.
5. *Ibid.,* vol. 1, page 631, col. 1, and footnote.
6. *Midrash Rabbah* on Leviticus, chap. 1, sect. 5 (page 10).
7. *Pesikta Rabbati,* piska 30, sect. 4 (vol. 2, page 597).
8. *Ibid.,* piska 44, sect. 19, (vol. 2, page 780).
9. *Ibid.,* piska 46, sect. 3 (vol. 2, page 792).
10. *The Jewish Encyclopedia,* vol. 8, page 465, col. 1.
11. *The Universal Jewish Encyclopedia,* vol. 7, art. "Metatron," page 507, col. 2.
12. BT *Abodah Zarah* 3b, page 10, footnote no. 6.
13. *The Encyclopedia Judaica,* vol. 11, page 1444.
14. *The Universal Jewish Encyclopedia,* vol. 7, page 507, col. 2.

Chapter 9

THE DEATH OF MOSES

AS THE fortieth year of Israel's wanderings in the wilderness drew near its end after their exodus from Egypt, so did the 120th year of the life of Moses, the great leader of his people, come to an end. He was not permitted to lead his people into the Promised Land of Canaan, but he was privileged to "see the land afar off" from the top of a peak, one of the highest points of Mount Nebo. Deuteronomy 32:52; 34:1.

The death and burial of Moses were unlike any other in human history. When he came to his end "his eye was not dim, nor his natural force abated." Verse 7. The burial was not performed with the usual pomp and ceremony given to kings and other leaders of nations. Instead of a funeral sermon, Moses delivered one of blessing for his people before bidding them farewell and going to the place of his death and burial. Chapter 33. We wonder if that vast multitude of Israelites, the whole nation assembled together at one place to hear him speak, really were aware of its significance, or knew that before the dawn of another morning he would be taken from them.

In all the history of Israel no other death and burial was like that of Moses. He was told, immediately after that last sermon of blessings, "Get thee up into this mountain of Abarim, unto mount Nebo, which is in the land of Moab, that is over against Jericho; and behold the land of Canaan, which I give unto the children of Israel for a possession; and die in the mount whither thou goest up, and be gathered unto thy people." Deuteronomy 32:49,50.

In obedience to that instruction, "Moses went up from the plains of Moab unto mount Nebo, to the top of Pisgah, that is over against Jericho. And the LORD showed him all the land, . . . And the LORD said unto him: 'This is the land which I

71

swore unto Abraham, unto Isaac, and unto Jacob, saying: I will give it unto thy seed; I have caused thee to see it with thine eyes, but thou shalt not go over thither.' So Moses the servant of the LORD died there in the land of Moab." Deuteronomy 34:1-5.

We try to picture in our imagination Moses finishing that last sermon of exhortation to Israel, and his turning away to walk alone toward the edge of the camp. We wonder what his final words to his wife and children were, and if they knew where he was going when he walked out of the camp after that remarkable sermon. He had put it in writing that he would not be permitted to enter the Promised Land. *Ib.* 32:51,52.

In the obituary notice penned for future generations to read, we find these remarkable words concerning that great man: "There hath not arisen a prophet since in Israel like unto Moses, whom the LORD [YHWH] knew face to face." *Ib.*34:10.

Concerning his burial we are told simply that "he was buried in the valley in the land of Moab over against Beth-peor; and no man knoweth of his sepulchre unto this day." Verse 6. No tombstone or other monument stands there to mark the place where his corpse was laid.

At Moses' Death

Tradition has handed down through the centuries some strange things about the death and burial of Moses. Concerning his interment, the Biblical record simply says: "He was buried in the valley in the land of Moab." Verse 6. We wonder who penned those words, inasmuch as no human being accompanied him to the place of his death and burial.

The Targum of Onkelos to Deuteronomy 34:6 says that "He [the Lord] buried him in the valley." The Jerusalem Targum and the Babylonian Talmud say the same thing.[1]

"Tall Tales"

The Targum of Palestine and some other rabbinical works of old tell some very "tall tales" about the death of Moses—that Michael and other celestial beings prepared an elaborate bed for Moses to die in, and that they carried him four miles to bury him in the valley.[2] Some went so far as to "declare that Moses never died."[3] Thus they contradict what the Holy Scriptures clearly teach.

The result of such unwarranted and fanciful teaching is well stated by a writer of modern times in the following words: "In the later legends the death of Moses is recounted more fantastically, with many marvelous details. But instead of the hero being glorified, as was certainly intended by these details, he is unconsciously lowered by some traits ascribed to him. He appears weak and fearsome, not displaying that grandeur of soul which he might reasonably have been expected to exhibit at his death."[4]

Moses Resurrected

On the other hand, several ancient rabbinical works tell us in modest terms that after his death Moses "ascended to heaven,"[5] "ascended on high,"[6] and "went to heaven riding on a cloud."[7] Also they speak of Moses as now being "in heaven."[8]

Likewise a spokesman for the great Messianic movement that originated with Jesus of Bethlehem in the first century C.E. stated in a letter that "Michael the archangel, when contending with the devil he disputed about the body of Moses, durst not bring against him a railing accusation, but said, The Lord rebuke thee." Jude 9. This agrees with the reports of three other leaders of the same movement who state that Moses appeared together with Elijah the prophet at the time of the transfiguration of Jesus one night in late summer in Galilee:

"After six days Jesus taketh Peter, James, and John his brother, and bringeth them up into a high mountain apart, and was transfigured before them: and his face did shine as the sun, and his raiment was white as the light. And, behold, there appeared unto them Moses and Elias talking with him." Matthew 17:1-3. See also Mark 9:2-4; Luke 9:23-30.

In that extraordinary experience Moses, having been resurrected from the grave, is generally regarded as a representative of all the righteous dead who will be resurrected from their graves when King Messiah comes to establish his kingdom upon the earth; and Elijah, who had been taken to heaven alive without having experienced death (2 Kings 2:1-14), is believed to be the representative of all the righteous who will be living and translated into the kingdom of the Messiah, without having died and experienced resurrection (See Daniel 12:1,2), when Messiah comes to reign as King of kings.

FOOTNOTES AND REFERENCES

1. BT *Sanhedrin* 38a (page 250); *Sotah* 13a (page 72).
2. *Midrash Rabbah* on Deuteronomy, chap. 11, sect. 10 pages 183-186.
3. BT *Sotah* 13b (page 72).
4. *The Jewish Encyclopedia,* vol. 9, pages 53, 54.
5. *Midrash Rabbah* on Deuteronomy, chap. 36, sect. 1 (page 64).
6. BT *Menahoth* 29b (page 190).
7. *The Midrash on Psalms,* Psalm 45, sect. 6 (vol. 1, page 453).
8. *Midrash Rabbah* on Deuteronomy, chap. 3, sect. 11 (page 78).

Chapter 10

MICHAEL AND JOSHUA

JOSHUA the son of Nun is first mentioned in Exodus 17:9-13, where he is reported to have been a loyal aide to Moses in directing the Israelite forces in repulsing a vicious attack by the Amalekites a few weeks after Israel had left Egypt. As the minister of Moses, Joshua accompanied him and the other Israelite leaders when they went up on the Mount Sinai for the ratification of the covenant made by God with Israel soon after He spoke the Ten Commandments. Exodus 24:13.

About a year later, when the Lord was ready for Israel to enter into the Land of Canaan, Joshua was one of the 12 men sent to spy out the Promised Land and bring back a report of the conditions there. Numbers 13:8. When the spies returned, only he and Caleb brought back an encouraging report. The other ten, lacking faith in God, brought back a discouraging report, and this caused Israel to rebel against the idea of attempting to possess the land. Numbers 14:1-10. As a result, Israel's entrance into the Promised Land was delayed approximately 38 years.

Shortly before the death of Moses, Joshua was formally installed by the laying on of hands in obedience to God's command, to be the successor of Moses as leader of the nation of Israel. Numbers 27:18-23.

Crossing the Jordan

In the spring season marking the close of the fortieth year of the exodus of Israel from Egypt, they were led to the eastern side of the Jordan River at a point near Jericho. At that time the river was overflowing its banks, as it usually did at that time of the year.[1]

At Gilgal on the west side of the Jordan, Israel encamped. There they celebrated the Passover on the 14th and 15th of Abib (Nisan). It was then that the manna ceased to be provided for the people, for they then began to eat of the grain crop of the land which was ripe at that time. Joshua 5:10-12.

Captain of the Lord's Host

The taking of Jericho, a strongly built and fortified key city of Canaan, was to be the first undertaking in Israel's occupation of the Promised Land. Prior to attempting to take that city, Joshua went outside the camp of Israel to meditate and pray that God would give them success.

When "he lifted up his eyes and looked, and, behold, there stood a man over against him with his sword drawn in his hand; and Joshua went unto him, and said unto him: 'Art thou for us, or for our adversaries?' And he said: 'Nay, but I am captain of the host of the LORD (YHWH); I am now come.' And Joshua fell on his face to the earth, and bowed down, and said unto him: 'What saith my lord unto his servant?' And the captian of the LORD's host said unto Joshua: 'Put off thy shoe from off thy foot; for the place whereon thou standest is holy.' And Joshua did so." Joshua 5:13-15.

That warrior of the highest rank, it should be noted, appearing in the guise of a man, was the celestial being whose holy presence sanctified the very ground on which He stood. He was none other than the divine Angel of the Lord who had appeared about forty years before to Moses at the burning bush near Mount Horeb. When He identified himself as the Captain of the Lord's host, Joshua had no scruples whatever against falling on his face immediately in worshipful submission to Him.

In comment on Joshua 5:13, a modern Jewish writer frankly acknowledges the fact that this was a "manifestation of the Lord, as is seen from Josh. vi. 2."[2]

The expression "captain of the host *(sar tseba)*" in Joshua 5:14,15 is strikingly similar to that of the "Prince of the host *(sar hats-tsaba')*" in Daniel 8:11, who is the "Prince of princes *(sar sarim)"* in verse 25 of the same chapter. Michael is "one of the chief princes *('echad has-sarim har-ri'shonim)."* and as such He is "the great Prince *(has-sar hag-gadol)* who standeth for the children of thy people." Daniel 10:13; 12:1.

The fact that the "Captain of the host of the Lord" is referred to as "a man" does not mean that he actually was a human being such as we are. On the contrary, it means that he appeared in the guise of a man, just as the celestial beings who appeared to Abraham at Mamre, as recorded in Genesis 18:2 are called "men"; and the heavenly being who wrestled with Jacob at Mahanaim (Peniel) appeared as a man. Genesis 32:25. The context in which the word "man" is used in Joshua 5:13 clearly indicates that this celestial being was far superior to any human being, and Joshua himself readily recognized him as such, and with his own tongue acknowledged that fact. Note these major facts that need to be considered in regard to this matter:

1. That person identified himself as "Captain of the host of the Lord."

2. Then Joshua "fell on his face to the earth, and bowed down" before him, which was a customary act of due respect and honor on the part of an inferior to a superior.

3. The superior One so honored told Joshua: "Put off thy shoe from off thy foot; for the place whereon thou standest is holy. And Joshua did so." Verse 15. That reminds us of what the Holy One said to Moses at the burning bush, as recorded in Exodus 3:5.

A widely used Jewish reference work had well said: "Joshua in front of Jericho receives the visit of a 'captain of the host of the Lord' in the guise of a man, who declares that the soil on which Joshua is standing is holy ground"[3]

The ancient Midrashic works contain the following statements concerning that experience of Joshua:

"R. Joshua said in the Name of R. Hanina b. Isaac: He cried out from his very toe-nails, *'I am captain of the host of the Lord'*; I am a prince of the celestial host, and wherever I appear the Holy One, blessed be He, appears."[4]

"Wherever the *Shechinah* appears one must not go about with shoes on; and so we find in the case of Joshua: *Put off thy shoe* (Josh. V. 15). Hence the priests ministered in the Temple, barefooted."[5]

Two Celestial Beings

It is quite obvious from verse 14 that two celestial beings are mentioned: (1) the "captain of the host of the Lord"; and (2) the LORD (YHWH) to whom the hosts belong.

Divine Encouragement

This wonderful experience must have reminded Joshua of this divinely inspired promise that Moses, shortly before his death, had given to him: "The LORD thy God, He will go over before thee; He will destroy these nations from before thee, and thou shalt dispossess them; . . . Be strong and of a good courage; for thou shalt go with this people into the land which the LORD hath sworn unto their fathers to give them; and thou shalt cause them to inherit it. And the LORD, He it is that doth go before thee; He will be with thee, He will not fail thee, neither forsake thee; fear not, neither be dismayed." Deuteronomy 31; 3,7,8.

FOOTNOTES AND REFERENCES

1. The flooding of the Jordan at this time of the year was a regular seasonal occurance (see 1 Chronicles 12:16), for melting snows of the mountains had caused the waters of the river to rise to flood stage. By a miracle of God, the surging waters of the stream were parted and the Israelite host marched across on dry ground, just as they had done through the Red Sea 40 years before. Joshua 3:14-17.
2. *The Jewish Encyclopedia,* vol. 1, page 589, col. 2.
3. *Ibid.,* vol. 7, page 284, col. 2.
4. *Midrash Rabbah* on Genesis, chap. 97, sect 3 (vol. 2, page 939).
5. *Ibid.,* on Exodus, chap. 2, sect. 6 (page 57).

Chapter 11

MICHAEL AND GIDEON

AGAIN we note the following statement found in one of Judaism's best known reference works: "In the earlier Biblical writings the term 'Malak YHWH' (messenger of the Lord) occurs chiefly in the singular, and signifies a special self-manifestation of God (see Gen. xxxi. 11-13, where the angel of God says, 'I am the God of Bethel; Ex. iii. 2-6, where the angel of the Lord who appeared to Moses in the flame of fire says, 'I am the God of thy father'; compare Gen. xxii. 11; Judges vi. 11-22). At times the angel clearly distinguishes himself from the Lord who sends him.'"[1]

At this point in our study of Israel's Angel extraordinary we turn our attention to Judges 6:11-22, mentioned in the quotation cited above. In order to fully appreciate what is said in that passage of Holy Scripture, we need to consider it in the light of its context. Verses 1-10 reveal that "the children of Israel did that which was evil in the sight of the Lord; and the Lord delivered them into the hand of Midian seven years. And the hand of Midian prevailed against Israel; and because of Midian the children of Israel made them the dens which are in the mountains, and the caves, and the strongholds. And so it was, when Israel had sown, that the Midianites came up, and the Amalekites, and the children of the east; they came up against them; and they encamped against them, and destroyed the produce of the earth, till thou come unto Gaza, and left no sustenance in Israel, neither sheep, nor ox, nor ass. For they came up with their cattle and their tents, and they came in as locusts for multitude; both they and their camels were without number; and they came into the land to destroy it. And Israel was brought very low because of Midian; and the children of Israel cried unto the Lord.

"And it came to pass, when the children of Israel cried unto the LORD because of Midian, that the LORD sent a prophet unto the children of Israel; and he said unto them: 'Thus saith the LORD, The God of Israel: I brought you up from Egypt, and brought you forth out of the house of bondage; and I delivered you out of the hand of the Egyptians, and out of the hand of all that oppressed you, and drove them out from before you, and gave you their land. And I said unto you: I am the LORD your God; ye shall not fear the gods of the Amorites, in whose land ye dwell; but ye have not hearkened unto My voice.'"

A Lesson For Us

These saddening, heart-rending words cannot rightly be construed as anti-Semitism. The Hebrew prophet who penned them was divinely inspired by the God of Israel, who loved His erring people. He had permitted them to suffer at the hands of their heathen enemies in order that they might see that He could not and would not bless and protect Israel when they would not hearken to His voice, but persisted in doing evil in His sight. The Lord our God has repeatedly told us in His Written Word that sin, the transgression of His law, leads to suffering and death. However, in His great love and mercy for His erring children our heavenly Father has repeatedly sent His prophets to warn them against their wrong-doing and to urge them to repent and return to Him.

After the death of Joshua, that great and faithful man who succeeded Moses as the chief magistrate in Israel, the nation fared remarkably well for a time. "Israel served the LORD all the days of Joshua, and all the days of the elders that outlived Joshua, and had known all the work of the LORD, that He had wrought for Israel." Joshua 24:31.

After the death of Joshua, and the elders who outlived him, there was a steady decline of love, loyalty, and obedience to God in Israel. However, there was a faithful remnant in every period of apostasy, and in this instance that was true.

While Gideon was concealing his harvest of grain at the winepress in his vineyard in order that enemy raiders might not find it, "the angel of the LORD came, and sat under the terebinth" near by him. Verse 11. The celestial visitor gave Gideon this assurance; " 'The LORD (YHWH) is with thee, thou mighty man of valor.' " Verse 12. Then he demonstrated his supernatural power in an astonishing, miraculous way in the presence of Gideon the peasant. Verses 16-23,

In the following night the Lord instructed Gideon to tear down the altar which his father had erected for the worship of Baal, the pagan sun god. This he did, and by that act was begun a religious reformation in Israel, with a partial restoration of the worship of the true God. He judged Israel 40 years.

Dr. A. Cohen, a Jewish scholar, in his book *Joshua and Judges,* has pointed out that "Commentators differ in their interpretation, some regarding the angel as identical with God (Rashi, Ralbag), and others distinguishing between them (as does the LXX)."[2]

Another Jewish scholar refers to Gideon's "divine visitor," and adds:"Gideon, reassured by YHWH that he will not die as a consequence of seeing His messenger (that is, YHWH Himself) face to face, builds an altar," etc.[3]

It is quite obvious that throughout the centuries of the past Michael was held in very high regard by many in Israel, among them religious teachers of good repute. His love for his people, and his interest in their spiritual well-being has been repeatedly manifested by his intervention in their behalf throughout the ages, and by his personal appearance to many of them to give counsel, instruction and guidance.

FOOTNOTES AND REFERENCES

1. *The Jewish Encyclopedia,* vol. 1, page 589, col. 1.
2. A. Cohen, *Joshua and Judges,* page 208.
3. *The Jewish Encyclopedia,* vol. 5, page 661, col. 1.

Chapter 12

MICHAEL OUR DELIVERER

MICHAEL, whose name means "Who Is Like God," was not only Israel's Angel extraordinary in ancient times, but he will continue to be so in our time and in the eternity yet to come. When he appeared to Joshua, who led Israel out of the wilderness of Sinai into the Land of Canaan to occupy it, Michael appeared to him as "Captain of the host of the Lord." Joshua 5:14. The Hebrew Word translated into English as "captain" in this instance is *sar*.

Centuries Later

Many centuries later the angel Gabriel appeared to Daniel, the Hebrew seer in far-away Babylon, at a very important point of time in the history of Israel. The 70 years of Babylonian captivity for the Jewish people were about to end, and the time for the fulfilment of the promise that God had made through Isaiah the prophet concerning Cyrus, the great king of Persia, had arrived. Isaiah 44:28; 45:1-5,13.

Belshazzar, a co-regent with his father King Nabonidus as ruler of Babylon, was publicly told in the midst of a great feast in his palace in Babylon: " 'Thy kingdom is divided, and given to the Medes and Persians.' " Daniel 5:28. Also it is recorded: "In that night Belshazzar the Chaldean king was slain." Verse 30.

Darius the Mede was the uncle of Cyrus the Great, king of Persia, who had taken the city of Babylon and placed him on the throne as ruler of the province. The year was 538 B.C.E.

The Decree of Cyrus

Somebody, probably Daniel himself, informed King Cyrus of what God had said through the prophet Isaiah concerning him more than 100 years before his birth. As a result, "In the first year of Cyrus king of Persia, that the word of the LORD by the mouth of Jeremiah might be accomplished, the LORD stirred up the spirit of Cyrus king of Persia, that he made a proclamation throughout all his kingdom, and put it also in writing, saying: 'Thus saith Cyrus king of Persia: All the kingdoms of the earth hath the LORD, the God of heaven, given me; And He hath charged me to build Him a house in Jerusalem, which is in Judah. Whosoever there is among you of all His people—his God be with him—let him go up to Jerusalem, which is in Judah, and build the house of the LORD, the God of Israel, He is the God who is in Jerusalem. And whosoever is left, in any place where he sojourneth, let the men of his place help him with silver, and with gold, and with goods, and with beasts, beside the freewill-offering for the house of God which is in Jerusalem.' " Ezra 1:1-4; 2 Chronicles 36:22,23.

This had been foretold also in the third year of the reign of Belshazzar king of Babylon. (See Daniel 8:1,4,20; 1:21; 10:1.) Daniel was an aged man at this time, but he still served as prime minister of the kingdom under the Persian regime. Daniel 6:2-4.

Michael's Role

It appears that King Cyrus was in a quandry for a period of a few weeks because of the adverse political influences, as to whether he should let the Jews return to their homeland (Daniel 10:13), and Daniel was in mourning and fasting, with prayer that God would interpose in behalf of His people. Gabriel, the holy angel who had attended Daniel in his ministry as God's seer, gave to him at this time some good news. God had heard the seer's prayer and gave to Gabriel this message for him: "Fear not, Daniel; for from the first day that thou didst set thy heart to understand, and to humble thyself before thy God, thy words were heard; and I am come because of thy words. But the prince of the kingdom of Persia withstood me one and twenty days; but, lo, Michael, one of the chief princes, came to help me; and I was left over there beside the kings of Persia. Now I am come to make thee understand what shall befall thy people in the end of the days." Daniel 10:12-14.

"One of the Chief Princes"

Note that Michael is referred to as "one of the chief princes." Gabriel explained to Daniel what had happened to cause the delay in the answer to his prayer, and added: "There is none that holdeth with me against these, except Michael your prince." Verse 21. Then Gabriel revealed to Daniel the course of the future history of the Land of Israel and its people down to "the time of the end." Daniel 10:14 to 12:4.

Gabriel explained that in these things he was working in close relationship with "Michael your prince." Daniel 10:21. That must have been a very cheering and encouraging message, not only for Daniel himself but also for the faithful in Israel as they were told what they must face during the centuries to come, as that prophetic message of Daniel 11 and 12 foretold.

Road Map for the Future

To Daniel the seer the Lord gave for Israel and the rest of mankind in Daniel 11 a prophetic road map of the future history of the world. He stated that there would yet be four more kings in Persia, and that the fourth one would be the richest of them all. Daniel 11:2. The Persian Empire lasted from 536 to 331 B.C.E. After that, the next empire would be Greece from 331 to 168 B.C.E. After the death of Alexander the Great in 323 B.C.E., the empire was broken up into four kingdoms of lesser size: (1) Egypt under Ptolemy; (2) Macedonia under Cassander; (3) Thrace and the western part of Asia Minor under Lysimachus; and (4) Syria and the eastward countries to the Indus under Seleucus Nicator. The Land of Israel was repeatedly a bone of political and military contention between Egypt and Syria thereafter.

In the battle of Pydna in northern Greece, the Roman armies won a great victory over the Greeks, and thereby became the imperial masters of the civilized world until 476 C.E. Then the empire was broken up into smaller nations, and from that time to the present it remained divided.

In the welter of it all little Israel, "the beauteous land" mentioned in Daniel 11:41,45, would be involved.

Michael Shall Stand Up

In the closing period of our sinful world's political history in that prophecy of Daniel, God will interpose and make some startling and radical changes. It is written that "At that time shall Michael stand up, the great prince who standeth for the children of thy people; and there shall be a time of trouble, such as never was since there was a nation even to that same time; and at that time thy people shall be delivered, every one that shall be found written in the book. And many of them that sleep in the dust of the earth shall awake, some to everlasting life, and some to reproaches and everlasting abhorrence. And they that are wise shall shine as the brightness of the firmament; and they that turn the many to righteousness as the stars for ever and ever." Daniel 12:1-3.

According to that sacred prediction, Michael, Israel's Angel extraordinary, has a major role to play soon in the history of our world. The God of Israel will not stand idly by and let the powers of evil wholly dominate our planet and establish upon it an everlasting kingdom of apostasy and wickedness. Michael, "the great prince which standeth for the children of thy people" (the true and faithful of all ages) will interpose and introduce a new order of things.

Then, for the first time, all the human beings who have lived upon the planet Earth will be assembled—both good and bad—by a mighty miracle of resurrection at the voice of Michael the archangel. The countless millions of dead people will come forth from their graves to stand before the Judge of all the earth, to be rewarded for good or bad as their works have been. The faithful of all ages since the time of Adam will be delivered, "every one that shall be found written in the book." Verse 1.

That day of destiny is not far off for the world of today. It will follow "a time of trouble, such as never was since there was a nation, even to that same time." Our greatly troubled world is already entering that "time of trouble," and we need to draw closer to God and faithfully conform to His prescribed way of life, in order that we may be delivered when His "people shall be delivered, every one that shall be found written in the book"—the Book of Life.

The role of Michael "the great prince which standeth for the children of thy people," who led Israel out of their bondage in Egypt to the Promised Land of Canaan, is yet to do something much greater than that. He will soon stand up and deliver the faithful of all ages, both the living and the dead, "every one found written in the book," and usher them into that everlasting kingdom of righteousness which will have no end.[1]

The Resurrection of the Dead

In our day it has been taught: "At the resurrection Michael will sound the trumpet, at which the graves will open and the dead will rise."[2]

Also: "The trumpet of resurrection, which will be followed by the opening of graves and the raising of the dead, is to be blown by Michael (*Othoth Hamashiah, in Jellinek, Beth Hamidrash,* vol. 2, pp. 61-62)."[3]

The adherents of the great Messianic (Christian) movement which had its beginning among the Jews of Palestine and spread into the rest of the civilized world in the first century C.E., taught that "the Lord himself shall descend from heaven with a shout, with the voice of the archangel, and with the trump of God: and the dead in Christ[4] shall rise first: then we which are alive and remain shall be caught up together with them in the clouds, to meet the Lord in the air: and so shall we ever be with the Lord." 1 Thessalonians 4:16,17.

Messianic Hope

A modern Jewish reference work twice refers to the prophecies of Isaiah 26:19 and Daniel 12:2 as of Messianic import for its readers, saying "Resurrection formed part of the Messianic hope (Isa. xxiv. 19; Dan. xii. 2)."[5]

The learned Dr. Judah J. Slotki has made this fitting comment on Daniel 12: "This chapter is generally taken by Jewish authorities to refer to the remote future which will herald the advent of the Messianic era."[6] An editorial footnote says: "*The end.* Until the Messianic era."[7]

Elsewhere we are told: "The old national point of view asserted itself in the form of Messianic hopes. These gave rise to a belief in a resurrection in order that more might share in the glory of the Messianic kingdom. This hope first finds expression in Isa. xxvi. 19 . . . The hope was cherished for faithful Israelites."[8]

Concerning the prophecy we are now considering, Dr. Joseph Klausner, who has written much about Israel's Messianic hope, has well said: "Almost all of Daniel is Messianic in spirit, but chapters 2, 6-9, and 12 are Messianic in essence."[9]

A Talmudic tractate penned long, long ago has pointed out that there would be no more communication by means of the Urim and Thumim "Until the dead revive and the Messiah, son of David comes!"[10]

It appears, therefore, that the time when Michael shall stand up and the resurrection of the dead shall take place, is the one when the Messiah will interpose in the affairs of our world to effect a very radical change in the course of human history. In fact, many are inclined to think that Michael, that celestial person whose name means "Who Is Like God" is the same one who is called the Messiah.

The belief that the resurrection of the dead will be effected by our long-awaited Messiah is not a new one. Israel has been told in a rabbinical work: "In the days of the Messiah the dead of the Land of Israel will be the first to come to life."[11]

It is said also: "In *My head is filled with dew* (Song 5:2), Scripture is alluding to the time of the Messiah, when, as the dead come back to life, the Messiah will be told 'Thy dew is as the dew of light, and the earth shall bring to life the shades' (Isa. 26:19).''[12]

Resurrection Denied

The people of Israel and their religious teachers have been sharply divided on the subject of the resurrection of the dead. Josephus, the noted historian of the Jewish Roman War that resulted in the destruction of Jerusalem and the Temple, and also the lives of more than a million Jews[13] in the years 66-70 C.E., was a well educated man of priestly rank. He was the commanding general of the Jewish troops in Galilee until he became a prisoner of the Romans. In his youth he made a careful study of the doctrines of the Sadducees, as well as those of the Essenes and the Pharisees, before he began to play his role as a military commander and historian of the nation.[14] Concerning the Sadducees, he says:

"The Sadducees hold that the soul perishes along with the body."[15] Elsewhere he says: "As for persistence of the soul after death, penalties in the underworld, and rewards, they [the Sadducees] will have none of them."[16]

It is acknowledged at the present time that in the first century C.E. the Sadducees rejected the doctrine of the resurrection of the dead. For example, it is said: "They [the Sadducees] would not accept the Pharisaic doctrine of the resurrection (Sanh. 90b; Mark XII. 12; Ber. ix. 5, 'Minim'), which was a national rather than individual hope."[17]

The Gospel of Mark, a document penned in the first century C.E., specifically mentions "the Sadducees, which say there is no resurrection." Mark 12:18. The Gospel of Matthew, written in the same century C.E., also mentions "the Sadducees, which say that there is no resurrection." Matthew 22:23. The Acts of the Apostles, which was penned in the same century, likewise states that "the Sadducees say that there is no resurrection, neither angel, nor spirit." Acts 25:8. The Gospel of Luke, written about the same time by the same writer, mentions "the

89

Sadducees, which deny that there is any resurrection." Luke 20:27.

In the Torah

This cleavage in doctrine among the people of Israel concerning the subject of the resurrection was a very serious one. It led to the Sanhedrin's adoption of the forthright statement concerning Israel's inheritance in the world to come: "The following have no portion therein: he who maintains that resurrection is not a Biblical doctrine," etc.[18]

It is equally interesting to note that the teachings of the Messianic (Christian) movement concerning the resurrection of the dead was in harmony with those of Israel's ancient prophets from Moses to Malachi. The leader of that movement declared: "Marvel not at this: for the hour is coming, in the which all that are in the graves shall hear his voice, and shall come forth; they that have done good, unto the resurrection of life; and they that have done evil, unto the resurrection of damnation." John 5:28,29.

And another writer stated: "For the Lord himself shall descend from heaven with a shout, with the voice of the archangel, and with the trump of God: and the dead in Christ shall rise first: then we which are alive and remain shall be caught up together with them in the clouds to meet the Lord in the air; and so shall we ever be with the Lord." 1 Thessalonians 4:16,17.

Also, the same writer said in another letter: "Behold, I show you a mystery; We shall not all sleep, but we shall all be changed, in a moment, in the twinkling of an eye, at the last trump: for the trumpet shall sound, and the dead shall be raised incorruptible, and we shall be changed. For this corruptible must put on incorruption, and this mortal must put on immortality. So when this corruptible shall have put on incorruption, and this mortal shall have put on immortality, then shall be brought to pass the saying that is written, Death is swallowed up in victory. O death, where is thy sting? O grave where is thy victory?" 1 Corinthians 15:51-55.

See also Hosea 13:14: "From the power of the grave would I ransom them, from death would I redeem them; (but now) where are thy plagues, O death, where is thy pestilence, O grave?" Hosea 13:14, Isaac Leeser's translation.

Not in the Torah?

Those religious teachers who in Israel taught that there would be no resurrection of the dead strongly insisted that no such promise could be found in the Torah, the Pentateuch penned by Moses.

For example, in a Talmudic tractate we read: "R. Eliezer, son of R. Jose, said: In this matter I refuted the books of the sectarians, who maintained that resurrection is not deducible from the Torah. I said to them: You have falsified your Torah, yet it has availed you nothing. For ye maintain that resurrection is not a Biblical doctrine."[19]

Another Talmudic tractate mentions "those who maintain that resurrection is not intimated in the Torah,"etc.[20]

It is quite obvious that the doctrine that there will be no resurrection of the dead, not even of the faithful ones, must have been a shocking message for many in Israel. We wonder how many faithful religious leaders opposed that teaching. We find it recorded that there were some men of courage and ability who taught and defended the doctrine of the resurrection of the dead by means of the Holy Scriptures, keen logic, and love for God and His Written Word. In one Talmudic tractate we find this statement:

"Whence do we know that the Holy One, blessed be He, will resurrect the dead? He answered them from the Torah, the Prophets, and the Hagiographa, yet they did not accept it [as conclusive proof]. 'From the Torah': for it is written, *And the Lord said unto Moses, Behold, thou shalt sleep with thy fathers and rise up* [again] [Deut. XXXI, 16]. 'But perhaps,' said they to him, '[the verse reads], *and the people will rise up'?* 'From the prophets': as it is written, *Thy dead men shall live, together with my dead body shall they arise. Awake and sing, ye that dwell in the dust: for the dew is as the dew of herbs, and the earth shall cast out its dead* [Isa. XXVI, 19]."[21]

"R. Simai said: Whence do we learn resurrection from the Torah?—From the verse, *And I also have established my covenant with them* [sc. the Patriarchs] *to give them the land of Canaan* [Ex. VI, 4]: '*[to give]* you' is not said, but '*to give* them' [personally]; thus resurrection is proved from the Torah."[22] The editorial footnote aptly comments: "The promise could be literally fulfilled only by the Patriarchs' resurrection."[23]

The statement of Moses in Exodus 6:2-4 clearly states: "And God spoke unto Moses, and said unto him: 'I am the LORD; and I appeared unto Abraham, unto Isaac, and unto Jacob, as God Almighty, but by My name YHWH I made Me not known to them. And I have also established My covenant with them, to give them the land of Canaan, the land of their sojournings, wherein they sojourned."

Note particularly that the God of Israel was speaking to Moses, the great prophet who wrote the Book of Exodus. Dare we presume to say that Moses lied when he wrote that? or that God lied to Moses when he said that? When those words were spoken by the God of Israel to Moses the patriarchs Abraham, Isaac, and Jacob had long been dead. Abraham's sole possession in the Land of Canaan was the cave of Machpelah, near Hebron (Mamre). When he died he was buried there with his wife Sarah.[24] Likewise Isaac and Jacob and their wives were buried there.[25]

Those of us who have visited that tomb near Hebron can not forget the pleasure with which the people there have shown us the resting place of those great patriarchs of Israel. This brought to my mind the promise made by God to Abraham during his sojourn of 100 years in the land of Canaan before he was laid in the tomb.

Soon after Lot separated from Abraham the Lord said: "Arise, walk through the land in the length of it and in the breadth of it; for unto thee will I give it." Genesis 13:17. Note particularly the promise concerning the land: "*Unto thee* will I give it." That partiarch died nearly 4000 years ago, and all that he had possessed of the land of Canaan was the cave-tomb that he bought near Mamre (Hebron). This imples that Abraham will receive it after his resurrection from the grave. The Targums of Onkelos and Palestine both concur with this statement quoted from Genesis 13:17.

In Genesis 17:7,8 that promise was repeated in these words: *"I will give unto thee,* and to thy seed after thee, the land of thy sojournings, all the land of Canaan, for an everlasting possession."* The Targums concur with that text in their interpretation of it.

To Isaac, the son of Abraham, the Lord said concerning the Land of Canaan: *"Unto thee,* and unto thy seed, I will give all these lands."* Genesis 26:3. The Targum of Onkelops agrees with that statement in the Holy Writ.

When the patriarch Jacob left home to escape the wrath of Esau, his father Isaac prayed that *"thou* mayest inherit the land of thy sojournings, which God gave unto Abraham."* Genesis 28:4. And when Jacob stopped for sleep at night at Bethel, the Lord said to him in a dream: "The land whereon thou liest, to thee will I give it, and to thy seed." Verse 13. The patriarch was then about 76 years old and still unmarried. Both Targums concur with that rendering of the text. When Jacob died at the age of 147 years he was in Egypt, but his corpse was taken to the cave of Machpela in the Land of Canaan for burial there.[25]

That promise, like those made to Abraham and Isaac as mentioned above, was made to Jacob personally. This implies that his resurrection from the dead will take place in order for him to inherit the Promised Land of Canaan and live in it forever.

When the time finally came for the exodus of Israel from Egypt to the Promised Land of Canaan, the Lord reminded Moses of the promise which He had made to Abraham, Isaac, and Jacob *"to give them* the Land of Canaan, the land of their sojournings."* Exodus 6:2-4. This imples that they will be raised from the grave to live again and receive the Promised Land. They did not receive it in their lifetime. The Targums in this instance also concur with the Mosaic text.

After their exodus from Egypt, and while they wandered in the wilderness en route to the Land of Canaan, Moses reminded them that the Lord would give them "all the land which He promised to give unto thy fathers." Deuteronomy 19:8. Here, too, the Targums concur. Thus we have again implied assurance of the resurrection of the dead which would make it possible for them to live again and possess the Promised Land.

Similarly in Nehemiah 9:23 the same assurance is reiterated. In Nehemiah's time Abraham, Isaac, and Jacob, the fathers of the Hebrew people, were still in the grave.

The adherents of the great Messianic (Christian) movement that began among the Jews in Palestine to spread far and wide throughout the world during the first century C.E., firmly held and taught the same doctrine. They taught concerning the faithful in Israel during the centuries since the time of Abraham: "These all, having obtained a good report through faith, received not the promise: God having provided some better thing for us, that they without us should not be made perfect." Hebrews 11:39,40.

That is a wonderful privilege that we may have, and it should inspire us to be faithful in order that we may enter into the promised land of the Better World to Come.

At a time when there was controversy among Israel's religious teachers concerning this subject, able men stood firm for the truth as it is recorded in Holy Writ. Here is an example of it:

"[Thus he [R. Johanan] did not satisfy them] until he quoted this verse, *which the Lord sware unto your fathers to give* to them (Deut. XI, 21); not to you, but *to them* is said; hence resurrection is derived from the Torah. Others say that he proved it from this verse, *but ye that did cleave unto the Lord your God are alive every one of you this day* (Ibid. IV, 4); just as you are all alive today, so shall you all live again in the world to come."[26]

When?

When will the ancient patriarchs and all the others faithful to the God of Israel, who is the Creator of all mankind, inherit the land promised to them by God? It will be after Michael shall stand up at the "time of the end" (Daniel 12:1-4), as we have noted above in our consideration of the 12th chapter of Daniel. The Lord has made it very clear that the time is coming when "the God of heaven" shall "set up a kingdom, which shall never be destroyed; nor shall the kingdom be left to another people; it shall break in pieces and consume all these kingdoms, but it shall stand for ever." Daniel 2:44.

Elsewhere it is said that after the great judgment foretold in Daniel 7:9,10, there will be given to the "one like unto a son of man" "dominion, and glory, and a kingdom, that all the peoples, nations, and languages should serve him; his dominion is an everlasting dominion, which shall not pass away, and his kingdom that which shall not be destroyed." Verse 14.

It is then that "the kingdom and the dominion, and the greatness of the kingdoms under the whole heaven, shall be given to the people of the saints of the Most High; their kingdom is an everlasting kingdom, and all dominions shall serve and obey them." Verse 27.

According to the prophecies in which those promises are made, we are near the "time of the end" mentioned in Daniel 12:4.

The God of Israel has assured us that when He created our world, "not for naught did He create it, to be inhabited did he form it." Isaiah 45:18, Leeser's translation.

The Lord has told us: "Behold, I create new heavens and a new earth; and the former things shall not be remembered, nor come into mind. But be ye glad and rejoice for ever in that which I create; for, behold, I create Jerusalem a rejoicing, and her people a joy. And I will rejoice in Jerusalem, and joy in My people; and the voice of weeping shall be no more heard in her, nor the voice of crying." Isaiah 65:17-19.

"For as the new heavens and the new earth, which I will make, shall remain before Me, saith the LORD, so shall your seed and your name remain. And it shall come to pass, that from one new moon to another, and from one Sabbath to another, shall all flesh come to worship before Me, saith the Lord." Isaiah 66:22,23.

In preparation for that better world to come, there will be a resurrection of the faithful who have died on earth, as foretold in Ezekiel 37:1-26. Then will be fulfilled the promises made in Psalm 37:9-11,20-22,28,29.

In all this, we must keep in mind the climax of the sinful history of humanity, as pictured prophetically in Daniel 12, where it is said: "At that time shall Michael stand up, the great prince who standeth for the children of thy people; and there shall be a time of trouble, such as never was since there was a nation, even to that same time; and at that time thy people shall be delivered, every one that shall be found written in the book." Verse 1.

That same Angel extraordinary who led Israel out of Egyptian slavery to the Promised Land of Canaan is the same one who will deliver the faithful of all ages—even those who are asleep in their graves—out of this troubled world into that Better World to Come, as promised so often in the Sacred Scriptures. Just before that deliverance takes place, there will be "a time of trouble, such as never was since there was a nation," which reminds us that Israel was delivered from Egyptian bondage after that nation had passed a time of trouble—the outpouring of ten terrible plagues in succession. That was a time of trouble such as Israel and Egypt had never experienced.

Only those who believed the word of God sent them through His prophet, and faithfully obeyed it, were delivered and privileged to cross over the Jordan and enter the Land of Promise. How faithful we ought to be in order that we may, with the faithful patriarchs of old, be ready to enter the Heavenly Canaan when Michael stands up to deliver his people, "every one that shall be found written in the book"—the Book of Life.

FOOTNOTES AND REFERENCES

1. See Daniel 2:44; 7:14,21,27.
2. *The Jewish Encyclopedia,* vol. 8, page 537, col. 2.
3. *The Universal Jewish Encyclopedia,* vol. 7, page 529, col. 2.
4. Here the word "Christ" is the English equivalent of the Greek term *Christos,* which is the Greek equivalent of the Hebrew term *Mashiach,* used 37 times in the Hebrew text of the Holy Scriptures. Its general meaning is "anointed." In Daniel 9:25 it is rendered as "one anointed," and in verse 26 as "an anointed one" in specific prophetic reference to Israel's promised Messiah. In the Greek translation (LXX), made by a large group of Jewish scholars during the reign of Ptolemy II (Philadelphus, king of Egypt, 309-246 B.C.E.), the Greek term *Christos* was employed as the equivalent of *Mashiach.* Hence, one of the leading exponents of the great Messianic movement (Christian) of the first century C.E. speaks about "the Messias, which is, being interpreted, the Christ." John 1:41; and again in John 4:25: "Messias cometh, which is called Christ." In these two instances the Aramaic equivalent is Messias, for the Aramaic language was in common use in Israel at that time. In modern English the word "christen," meaning "anoint," is still in common use.
5. *The Jewish Encyclopedia,* vol. 5, page 216, col. 1; vol. 10, page 383, col. 2. *Note:* The Scripture reference given to support that statement is mistakenly given as Isaiah 24:19, but the correct reference should have been Isaiah 26:19.
6. Judah J. Slotki, *Daniel, Ezra, and Nehemiah,* pages 100, 101.
7. *Ibid.,* page 102, footnote no. 4.
8. *The Jewish Encyclopedia,* vol. 10, page 382, col. 1.
9. Joseph Klausner, *The Messianic Idea in Israel,* page 228.
10. BT *Sotah* 48b (page 259).
11. *Pesikta Rabbati,* Piska 1, sect. 4 (vol. 1, page 42).
12. *The Midrash on Psalms,* Psalm 18, sect. 11 (vol. 1, page 241).
13. Josephus, *War,* bk. 6, chap. 9, sect. 3 (lines 420, page 497, HUP edition).
14. See Josephus, *Life,* sect. 2, (HUP, *Josephus,* vol. 1, page 5, lines 7-12).
15. *Ibid., Antiquities,* book 18, chap. 1, sect. 4, (HUP *Josephus,* vol. 9, page 13, lines 16).
16. *Ibid., War,* book 2, chap. 8, sect. 14, (lines 165, 166. HUP, vol. 2, page 387.
17. *The Jewish Encyclopedia,* vol. 10, page 631. col. 2. *Note:* The Mark 12:12 reference is incorrect. It should be Mark 12:18.
18. BT *Sanhedrin* 90a (page 601). *Note:* It is astonishing that there should have existed in Israel nineteen centuries ago such confusion and contradiction concerning the teaching of Holy Writ about the resurrection of the dead as that which is recorded in BT *Kethuboth* 111a and b (pages 716-719); and *Sotah* 5a (page 19).
19. BT *Sanhedrin* 90b (page 606).
20. BT *Pesahim* 68a (page 347).
21. BT *Sanhedrin* 90b (pages 604, 605).
22. *Ibid.,* page 604.
23. *Ibid.,* footnote no. 10.
24. Genesis 23:3-20; 25:8-10.

25. Genesis 49:28-32; 50:4-13.
26. BT *Sanhedrin* 90b (page 605).

Chapter 13

A HEAVENLY SANCTUARY

APPROXIMATELY 1800 years before the second Temple was destroyed by the Romans in 70 C.E., the patriarch Abraham led a band of 318 trained men to rout in a night battle a foreign army that had looted Sodom and other cities in eastern Canaan. Genesis 14:14. When the patriarch returned with the loot that he had taken from the invaders he was met by Melchizedek king of Salem and a "priest of God the Most High." Genesis 14:18. Moreover, Abraham gave to that priest of the Most High a tenth of all the spoils taken in the war.

That story is an interesting one, and it is strange that we hear or read today so little about that notable king-priest Melchizedek. It is a noteworthy fact that there existed such a God-fearing king-priest in Canaan in Abraham's time, when idolatry was so widespread in that land. That explains, perhaps, why the Lord told Abraham that the occupation of Canaan by his descendants would not take place until 400 years later, "for the iniquity of the Amorites is not yet full." Genesis 15:13-16. It was not until the reign of King David (1011-971 B.C.E.) that Salem, then a Jebusite stronghold, was taken by military forces, and its name changed from Salem to Jerusalem.[1]

Israel's Mission

Israel's divinely appointed mission in the world was primarily a religious one. When He took them into covenant relationship with Himself at Mount Sinai, the Lord declared: "Ye shall be unto Me a kingdom of priests, and a holy nation." Exodus 19:6. Through one of His prophets the Lord later reminded them of this, saying: "For the priest's lips should keep knowledge, and they should seek the law at his mouth; for he is the messenger of the Lord of hosts." Malachi 2:7.

While Israel was encamped at Mount Sinai, the Lord endeavored to prepare His people to fulfil that sacred mission to the world and thereby become a blessing to "all the families of the earth,"[2] as He had declared to Abraham, Isaac, and Jacob.

Besides giving to Israel the Torah while they were encamped at Mount Sinai, He said also to them: "Let them make Me a sanctuary, that I may dwell among them." Exodus 25:8. It was a portable structure approximately 55 feet long, about 18 feet wide, and about 18 feet high. It could be dismantled and reassembled as needed when they moved from place to place. It was the center of public worship in Israel during the 480 years (1 Kings 6:1) preceding the building of the Temple in the fourth year of the reign of King Solomon (971-931 B.C.E.) That portable tabernacle was to be an object lesson to the people, and the various religious services and ceremonies connected with it were to serve as a means of illustrating God's plan for the salvation of mankind from sin and its consequences.

A Typical Establishment

The portable sanctuary built in the camp of Israel during the first year of their exodus from Egypt consisted of three principal parts: (1) the large court which surrounded it, (2) the first apartment of the tabernacle itself, which was about 36 feet long and was called the Holy Place; and (3) the innermost apartment, about 18 feet square, which was called the Most Holy Place. In the court was the altar of burnt offerings, where the sacrificial animals were slain. In the first apartment of the sanctuary proper were the seven-branched candlestick on the south side, and the table of showbread on the north side, while the golden altar of incense stood midway between the walls and in front of the veil that divided the sanctuary into two apartments.

In the court and in the first apartment of the sanctuary the priests performed the daily ministry for the people. On the Day of Atonement every year the high priest performed his special ministry for the people in the Most Holy Place. In this second apartment was located the ark of the covenant which contained the two tables of stone on which were written the Ten Commandments. Upon the cover of the ark stood two golden cherubim with outstretched wings, and their faces looking downward toward the mysterious light, called the Shekinah, which symbolized the Divine Presence.

The Antitype

When the Lord gave to Moses detailed instructions concerning the building of the tabernacle, He said: "See that thou make them after their pattern, which is being shown thee in the mount." Exodus 25:40. This included also all the furniture within the building: "the pattern of all the furniture thereof, even so shall ye make it." Verse 9. See also Numbers 8:4.

The Temple on Earth

When King David gathered material for the building of the Temple in Jerusalem, he "gave to Solomon his son the pattern of all that he had by the Spirit, for the courts of the house of the Lord, and for all the chambers round about, for the treasuries of the house of God, and for the treasuries of the hallowed things." 1 Chronicles 28:11,12.

Note especially that the pattern for the building of the Temple and its furnishings were revealed to David by the Spirit of the Lord. Thus both the portable tabernacle and the Temple which replaced it were patterned after something which God had revealed to Moses and David. This idea is well put in a Midrashic treatise: "He [God] then showed a model to Moses."[3]

The Temple in Heaven

According to what we have considered above, Israel's portable tabernacle and the Temples which replaced it later, were patterned after the heavenly one which was shown to Moses and to David respectively as the model for the building of the earthly one. Josephus, the Jewish historian who lived and wrote in the first century C.E., was a son of Matthias, a priest of the first of the 24 courses that served at the Temple. He was born in 37/38 C.E.[4] In his history of the Jewish people he says this concerning the corner pillars which supported the tabernacle built in the time of Moses:

"The area within these pillars was the sanctuary; the rest of the tabernacle was open to the priests. Now this partitionment of the tabernacle was withal an imitation of universal nature; for the third part of it, that within the four pillars, which was inaccessible to the priests, was like heaven devoted to God, while the twenty cubits' space, even as earth and sea are accessible to men, was in like manner assigned to the priests alone."[5]

That shows, too, that he believed that the earthly sanctuary (the Temple) symbolized the greater and far superior one which embraced both heaven and earth in the purposes of God. First the court of the earthly sanctuary was the one where the animal sacrifices were slain to atone for the sins of the people. It represents our world. It is here that the repentant sinner must confess his sin, turn from it, and await the day of final judgment. The two apartments of the earthly sanctuary symbolized the heavenly one in which God, the Judge of all men, receives the sinner's confession of sin and his petition for pardon and mercy, just as the earthly priest presented the blood of the sin offering within the earthly tabernacle proper as a sign of the confessor's repentance and plea for forgiveness. Thus the two apartments of the earthly tabernacle are likened by Josephus to "heaven devoted to God."

As one Talmudic statement puts it: "The earthly Temple corresponds to the heavenly Sanctuary."[6]

The following Talmudic statement makes it clear that there was belief in the existence of two separate and distinct sanctuaries, (1) the earthly and (2) the heavenly:

"In the Mishna it is said: That he who cannot turn himself should address his thoughts towards the Holy of Holies. Of which Holy of Holies does it speak? According to R. Hiya Raba's opinion, it means the heavenly Holy of Holies; according to that of R. Shimon, son of Halaphta, it refers to the earthly Holy of Holies; and R. Pinhas remarks: These two Rabbis do not dispute; the earthly Holy of Holies (in Jerusalem) is just under the heavenly Holy of Holies."[7]

A Midrashic statement on this subject says: "Precious in God's sight was the construction of the ark even as that of the Throne of Glory in heaven; as it says: *The place, O Lord, which Thou hast made for Thee to dwell in, the Sanctuary, O Lord, which Thy hands have established* (Ex. xv, 17). The [position of the terrestrial] Sanctuary corresponds with that of the heavenly Sanctuary and the [position of the] ark with that of the heavenly Throne."[8]

"This refers to the celestial Holy of Holies, which is exactly oposite *(mekuwan)* the lower holy of holies, as it says, *The place* (makon) . . . *for Thee to dwell in* (Ex. xv, 17)—that is, exactly opposite to Thy dwelling place."[9] The editorial footnote to that passage says: "The Rabbis held that there was a celestial Temple corresponding to the earthly one."[10]

Another Midrashic work is very clear in saying that the earthly sanctuary was a counterpart of the heavenly one: "R. Hisda said: There is no difference of opinion that the sanctuary below is the counterpart of the sanctuary above, for in the verse *Thou, Lord, hast made it a place (mkwn) for Thy dwelling* (Ex. 15:17) you are to read not *mkwn* 'a place for,' but *mekuwwan* 'a counterpart of.' "[11]

This raises an interesting question, which is this: Who is the high priest of the Sanctuary (the Temple) in heaven, the one who ministers there in our behalf?

The answer to this question is presented in the next chapter of this book.

FOOTNOTES AND REFERENCES

1. See 2 Samuel 5:6-10; 1 Chronicles 11:4-8.
2. Genesis 12:3; 18:18; 22:18; 26:4; 28:14.
3. *Midrash Rabbah* on Numbers, chap. 15, sect. 10 (vol. 2, page 650).
4. Josephus, *Life,* chap. 1, sect. 1 (HUP *Josephus,* vol. 1, lines 1-5, pages 3-5).
5. *Ibid., Antiquities,* bk. 3, chap. 6, sect. 4, page 375, lines 123 (HUP vol. 4, page 375).
6. BT *Haggigah* 12b (page 70), footnote no. 2.

7. JT vol. 1, *Berakhoth,* chap. 4, sect. 5 (pages 92, 93).
8. *Midrash Rabbah* on Numbers, chap. 4, sect. 13 (vol. 1, page 110).
9. *Ibid.,* on Song of Songs, chap. 3, sect. 10 (page 170).
10. *Ibid.,* footnote no. 3. See also *Ibid.,* page 197.
11. *The Midrash on Psalms,* Psalm 30, sect. 1, (vol. 1, page 386).

Chapter 14

OUR HEAVENLY HIGH PRIEST

NEARLY 900 years after the patriarch Abraham offered a ram instead of his son Isaac as a sacrifice on the altar he built on Mount Moriah, the divinely inspired psalmist wrote this very significant statement: "The LORD saith unto my lord: 'Sit thou at My right hand, until I make thine enemies thy footstool.' . . . The LORD hath sworn, and will not repent: 'Thou art a priest for ever after the manner of Melchizedek.' " Psalm 110:1,4.

That reference to Melchizedek reminds us of Abraham's acquaintance with "Melchizedek king of Salem," who was also "priest of God the Most High." Genesis 14:18.

Isaac Leeser's translation is more correct in rendering Psalm 110:4 as saying: "The Lord hath sworn, and will not repent of it, Thou shalt be a priest for ever after the order of Malki-zedek."

To whom was the LORD (YHWH) speaking when He made that statement? He was speaking to the person whom the psalmist called "my lord" in verse 1. Some rabbis of old have maintained that the promise was made to Abraham,[1] who had been dead and buried in the tomb of Machpelah many centuries before. It is inconceivable that God would be speaking to a person long dead. Others maintained that he was Shem, Noah's son, who died about 150 years after Abraham was born.[2]

Melchizedek

It is said that "Michael is identified with Melchizedek ('Yalk. Hadash,' 'Mal'akim,' No. 19)."[3]

The person whom the psalmist calls "my lord" in verse 1 is not specifically identified by name in Psalm 110. He is described in verse 4 as one to whom the LORD (YHWH) has said "Thou art a priest for ever after the manner of Melchizedek." According to Genesis 14:18, the man Melchizedek held two high offices: (1) "king of Salem" and (2) "priest of God the Most High." Thus we conclude from Psalm 110 that the psalmist's "lord" was an important person divinely appointed to serve as a king-priest "after the manner of Melchizedek." This means that he did not become a king-priest by heredity. That is to say, he did not become king-priest by right of hereditary descent from a succession of ancestors who were priest-kings.

In patriarchal times men did become by descent priestly rulers. Abraham was the chief ruler and priest of his household; when he died that office passed to Isaac, and from Isaac it passed to Jacob. Before he died, Jacob made a change in that matter. Because of his sinful conduct, Reuben, as the firstborn son of Jacob, forfeited the privileges of the birthright which otherwise would have been his at his father's death.[4] Consequently, Jacob bestowed upon Joseph and his two sons the birthright double portion of wealth.[5] Upon his son Judah Jacob bestowed the birthright title of leadership.[6] Later, the birthright of the priesthood was given to Levi and his tribe.[7]

Thus the person designated as king-priest in Psalm 110 received his office as such by direct appointment from the LORD (YHWH) as Melchizedek had received his, and not by inheritance. The priesthood in Israel was a hereditary office by descent from Aaron, a member of the tribe of Levi. The right of kingly office was hereditary by descent from King David, a member of the tribe of Judah.

In the case of the person mentioned in Psalm 110, he is made a "priest for ever." That is, he would hold that office throughout the eternal ages to come, and he would not be succeeded at any time by another. The priestly office in ancient Israel was a hereditary one, and only a male descendant of Aaron of the tribe of Levi could occupy it. This meant that a genealogical record of Aaron's male descendants must be kept and preserved throughout the generations from the time of Aaron onward. In the case of Melchizedek, there is no mention of his holding the office of priest by hereditary right. No mention is made of either his father or his mother. He must have held that office of "priest of God the Most High" by divine appointment.

Furthermore, in the case of the king-priest in Psalm 110, he was told by the LORD Himself: " 'Sit thou at My right hand, until I make thine enemies thy footstool.' " Verse 1. When a person sat at the right hand of a supreme ruler in ancient times, it meant that he occupied a position of high authority and honor next to that of the person who appointed him to it.

In reference to Abraham, Josephus says that "he was received by the king of Solyma, Melchisedek; this name means 'a righteous king,' and such was he by common consent, insomuch that for this reason he was moreover made priest of God; Solyma was in fact the place afterwards called Hierosolyma."[8]

Michael at God's Right

It is not surprising that in time past in their teaching concerning God the rabbis mentioned "Michael at His right."[9]

Hence a modern Jewish reference work tells its readers that "Michael is on the right of God's throne," etc.[10]

Michael as Priest

The concept of Michael as a priest in the heavenly sanctuary has been in vogue for centuries. In modern times he is represented as being "the prince or advocate of Israel."[11] Again: "The conception of Michael as an advocate always interceding on behalf of Israel gave rise to another idea, that of his being a high priest making atonement for his people."[12]

It is taught today that "Michael is Israel's representative in heaven."[13] Another modern work explains: "He [Michael] was regarded as the angel of mercy, and some mystics envisioned him as serving as a heavenly high priest."[14]

Also "Michael . . . is frequently referred to as high priest."[15]

It is said of those who built the Temple in the reign of King Solomon (971-931 B.C.E): "They saw [in a vision] the altar built, and Michael the great prince standing and offering upon it."[16]

Two other Talmudic works of long ago are cited to support that historic concept, as follows: "An altar has even been erected in heaven on which the angel Michael sacrifices (Men. 110a; Hag. 13b)."[17] Again: "In Hag. 12b it is stated that there is in heaven a Jerusalem, containing a sanctuary in which Michael, the great prince, stands like the high priest on earth, offering up sacrifice."[18]

The first-mentioned Talmudic work refers to "the altar built [in heaven], where Michael the great Prince, stands and offers up thereon an offering."[19]

The other Talmudic work affirms: "Zebul is that in which [the heavenly] Jerusalem and the Temple and the Altar are built, and Michael, the great Prince [Dan. XII, 1], stands and offers up thereon an offering, for it is said: *I have surely built Thee a house of habitation* [Zebul], *a place for Thee to dwell in for ever* [I Kings VIII, 13]."[20] The editorial footnote says: "The Holy One, blessed be He, said: I shall not enter the Jerusalem which is above, until I enter the Jerusalem which is below."[21]

People today are told: "Zebul, the upper Jerusalem, with its Temple, in which Michael offers the sacrifice at the altar (Isa. lxiii. 15; 1 Kings viii. 13)."[22] The Hebrew term *zebul* means "dwelling place" or "habitation."

Michael has been a very beloved celestial being among the faithful in Israel since the time of Abraham. A Midrashic work of old says this concerning him: "Just as God did in this world through the hand of Michael and Gabriel, so will He perform in the future also through them, for it says: *And Saviours shall come up on Mount Zion to judge the Mount of Esau (Obad. 1, 21)*—this refers to Michael and Gabriel. Our holy Teacher is of the opinion that this refers to Michael only, for it says: *And at that time shall Michael stand up, the great prince who standeth for the children of thy people* (Dan. 12:1), because he it is who presents Israel's requirements and pleads for them." Daniel 10:21 is quoted.[23]

The same work tells this tale concerning Michael and Samael (Satan): "R. Jose said: To what may Michael and Samael be compared? To an intercessor and an accuser before a tribunal." "So also do Michael and Samael both stand before the Divine Presence; Satan accuses, while Michael points out Israel's virtues," etc.[24]

It was taught in times past concerning the Jews in Persia in the time of Queen Esther when a plot was made to destroy them all throughout the empire on a certain day: "Michael pleaded a defence for them above."[25]

Another Midrashic work speaks of "the altar built in heaven, beside which Michael the great guardian angel stands and brings an offering."[26]

That Michael was regarded as the repentant sinner's friend is a precious thought expressed in this statement: "When Israel turns toward the Lord, his advocate, Michael, will plead in his favor (Pesik. R. 44 [ed. Friedmann, p. 185a])"[27]

The rabbinical work here cited says: "I would have your advocate, Michael, be your witness; as it is said *And at that time shall Michael stand up . . . who standeth for the children of thy people* (Dan. 12:1)."[28]

A currently published prayer book contains this plea for the observer to present in prayer on New Year's Day, according to the Jewish calendar: "May it be Thy will that the sounds of the Shofar (Ram's horn) which we have sounded today be woven into thy tapestry by the intercession of Elijah and by Yeshua, the Prince of Thy presence and Prince of might. So mayest Thou receive our pleas and extend to us Thy compassion."[29]

Messiah

More significant and interesting yet is the fact that teachers in Israel long ago taught that our Messiah is the person referred to in Psalm 110:1,4. In fact, Psalm 110:1 and Daniel 7:13,14 are linked together by ancient Israelite expositors in this manner: "In the decree of the Writings it is written, *The Lord said unto my lord: 'Sit thou at My right hand, until I make thine enemies thy footstool* (Ps. 110:1), and it is also written *I saw in the night visions, and, behold, there came with the clouds of heaven one like unto a son of man, and he came even to the Ancient of days, and he was brought near before Him. And there was given him dominion, and glory, and a kingdom, that all the peoples, nations, and languages should serve him* (Dan. 7:13,14).''[30]

"In another comment, the verse is read *I will tell of the decree: The Lord said unto me: Thou art My son . . . Ask of Me, and I will give the nations for thine inheritance, and the ends of the earth for thy possession* (Ps. 2:7,8). R. Yudan said: All these goodly promises are in the decree of the King, the King of kings, who will fulfill them for the lord Messiah."[31]

Again it is recorded that "R. Yudan said in the name of R. Hama: In the time-to-come, when the Holy One, blessed be He, seats the lord Messiah at His right hand, as is said *The Lord saith unto my lord: 'Sit thou at My right hand,'* (Ps. 110:1), and seats Abraham at His left, Abraham's face will pale, and he will say to the Lord: 'My son's son sits at the right, and I at the left!' Thereupon the Holy One, blessed be He, will comfort Abraham, saying: 'Thy son's son is at My right, but I, in a manner of speaking, am at thy right': *The Lord [is] at thy right hand* (Ps. 110:5).''[32]

A Talmudic writer has taught: "Similarly we find in the verse, *These are the two anointed ones that stand by the Lord of the whole earth* [Zech. IV, 14]; these are Aaron and the Messiah. I know not which of the two is the more beloved; when, however, Scripture states, *The Lord hath sworn and will not repent: Thou art a priest for ever [after the manner of Melchizedek]* [Ps. CX, 4], I know that the king Messiah is more beloved than the righteous priest."[33]

A modern Jewish writer refers to this text as a Messianic prediction. We read: "The Midrash (Tanhuma, Ps. 18, end of 29, ed. Buber p. 79) also gives a Messianic interpretation of Ps. CX: 'In the time to come God will seat the King Messiah on his right hand as it is written, The Lord said unto my Lord, sit on my right hand (Ps. cx. 1).' ''[34]

Now note Psalm 110:1: "The Lord said unto my Lord, Sit thou at my right hand, until I make thine enemies thy footstool." Here is God, speaking as a Father to the Messiah as His Son. It was so applied in the New Testament.[35]

Dr. Joseph Klausner, in citing the fact that Jesus, like an expert Pharisee, quoted Psalm 110:1, has commented: "In the Psalter is 'A Psalm of David' which Jesus, like every Jew of the time, accepted without question as written by David and referring to the Messiah."[36]

That led Dr. Klausner to ask: "How can David call the Messiah 'Lord,' when the Messiah is David's son?"[37] It is obvious from the statements in Micah 5:1; Isaiah 7:14; 9:5,6, that such a relationship could be established only by the Messiah's incarnation in human flesh as the result of a miraculous birth effected by the power of God. We must not scoff at the fact that our Creator, who created Adam a human being from the dust of the ground, will recreate or resurrect to life countless billions of human beings reduced to dust by death.

In the Midrashic Writings

A Midrashic writer says concerning the "staff' in Genesis 38:18: "AND THY STAFF alludes to the royal Messiah, as in the verse, *The staff of thy strength the Lord will send out of Zion* (Ps. 110:2)."[38]

The mention of Aaron's staff in Num. 17:21, reminded the sages of Ps. 110:2, as follows: "That same staff also is destined to be held in the hand of the King Messiah (may it be speedily in our days!); as it says, *The staff of thy strength the Lord will send out of Zion: Rule thou in the midst of thine enemies* (Ps. CX, 2)."[39]

One Midrashic writer went so far as to teach that "The Sanctuary was set upright in front of Him, and the name of the Messiah was engraved in a precious stone upon the altar."[40]

That Jewish doctrine concerning the Messiah, as foretold in Ps. 110:1-4, was accepted and taught also by the adherents of the great Messianic (Christian) movement which began in Israel and spread throughout the civilized world in the first century C.E. In fact, Yeshua (Jesus) himself called attention to the statement in Psalm 110.[41] Hence we are told: "In order to claim the priesthood for Jesus, early Christianity designated Him as

111

'after the order of Melchizedek' (Heb. 6:20).''[42]

Conclusion

The prophet Zechariah in the sixth century B.C.E. also foretold the dual role of Israel's promised Messiah as a king-priest, saying that "He shall bear the glory, and shall sit and rule upon his throne; and a priest shall be upon his own throne: and the counsel of peace shall be between both of them." Zechariah 6:13, Isaac Leeser's translation.

In the Hebrew text of Zechariah 6:13 the prophet literally says: He "shall sit and rule on His throne; and He shall be a priest on His throne; and the counsel of peace shall be between the two of them." That is, there would be no conflict or contradiction of purpose or action in the Messiah's dual role as a king-priest in carrying out God's plan for the redemption of man from sin. Thus the message of Zechariah the prophet is in complete harmony with that of Psalm 110:1,4.[43]

It has been well said that the Book of Zechariah the prophet "reiterates the promise of the Messiah (vi. 9-15)."[44]

Michael's priestly ministry in behalf of earth's repentant sinners is performed before God in the heavenly Sanctuary, which is the model after which the Mosaic Sanctuary and the Temple of Solomon were fashioned. When his priestly ministry there ends, the Messiah will come in glory as King of kings to destroy the impenitent and establish his everlasting kingdom upon the earth, as foretold in Daniel 7.

According to Psalm 110, Israel's promised Messiah as our king-priest, "after the manner of Melchizedek," occupies the position of highest honor next to the LORD (YHWH)—"at My right hand"—prior to the overthrow of his enemies. That is fully in harmony with what is taught in Daniel 7:9,13,14, where the Messiah, "the one like unto a son of man" is escorted in great pomp and glory into the Divine Presence, and brought near unto Him in the heavenly tribunal, prior to receiving his universal and everlasting dominion over the world. R. Akiba correctly taught that one of those "thrones" in Daniel 7:9 was for the

King Messiah,[45] the eternal son of King David and ultimate successor to his throne.

However, this world has not yet come to the time when the Messiah's enemies are made his footstool, and when "all the peoples, nations, and languages should serve him." Daniel 7:14. This means that we who are alive today have the opportunity to prepare for citizenship in Messiah's everlasting kingdom so soon to be established.

FOOTNOTES AND REFERENCES

1. See *Midrash Rabbah* on Genesis, chap. 46, sect. 5 (vol. 1, page 392); chap. 55, sects. 6,7 (pages 486, 488); on Leviticus, chap. 25, sect. 6 (page 320); on Deuteronomy, chap. 2, sect. 7 (page 35); BT *Nedarim* 32b (pages 98, 99 with footnote no. 6); *Sanhedrin* 108b (page 747, with footnote no. 3); *The Midrash on Psalms* 110 (vol. 2, pages 203-206)
2. See *The Jewish Encyclopedia,* vol. 8, page 450, col. 2; *Pirke de Rabbi Eliezer,* chap. 27 (pages 195, 196); Targum of Palestine to Genesis 14:4; *Midrash on Psalms,* Psalm 37, sect. 1 (vol. 1, page 422).
3. *The Jewish Encyclopedia,* vol. 8, page 537, col. 1.
4. Genesis 35:22; 49:3, 4.
5. Genesis 48:9-20.
6. Genesis 49:8-10.
7. Exodus 28:1; Deuteronomy 21:5.
8. *Antiquites,* bk. 1, chap. 10, sect. 2 (HUP *Josephus* vol. 4, lines 179, 180, page 89).
9. *Midrash Rabbah* on Numbers, chap. 2, sect. 10 (vol. 1, page 39) with footnote no. 4; *Pesikta Rabbati,* piska 46, sect. 3 (vol. 2, page 792); *Pirke de Rabbi Eliezer,* chap. 4, page 22.
10. *The Jewish Encyclopedia,* vol. 8, page 538, col. 1.
11. *Ibid.,* page 536, col. 1.
12. *Ibid.,* page 537, col. 1.
13. *Ibid.,* vol. 1, page 584, col. 2.
14. *The Universal Jewish Encyclopedia,* vol. 7, page 529.
15. *The Encyclopedia Judaica,* vol. 11, page 1490.
16. BT *Zebahim* 62a (page 305).
17. *The Jewish Encyclopedia,* vol. 10, page 625, col. 1.
18. *Ibid.,* vol. 1, page 587, col. 2.
19. BT *Menachoth* 110a (page 680).
20. BT *Hagigah* 12b (pages 69, 70).
21. *Ibid.,* Footnote no. 19.
22. *The Jewish Encyclopedia,* vol. 1, page 591, col. 2.
23. *Midrash Rabbah* on Exodus, chap. 18, sect. 5, (pages 221, 222).

24. *Ibid.*, (page 222).
25. *Ibid.*, on Esther, chap. 7, sect. 12 (page 91).
26. *The Midrash on Psalms,* Psalm 134, sect. 1 (vol. 2, page 321).
27. *The Jewish Encyclopedia*, vol. 8, page 537, col. 1.
28. *Pesikta Rabbati,* Piska 44, sect. 10 (vol. 2, page 780).
29. *Prayer Book for the New Year,* by A. Th. Philips, page 100.
30. *The Midrash on Psalms,* Psalm 2, sect. 9 (vol. 1, pages 40, 41).
31. *Ibid.*, (page 41).
32. *Ibid.,* Psalm 18, sect. 29 (vol. 1, page 261).
33. MTT *'Aboth D'Rabbi Nathan,* chap. 34, sect. 4 (vol. 1, page 164).
34. Joseph Klausner, *Jesus of Nazareth,* footnote to page 320.
35. Matthew 22:44; Acts 2:34,35.
36. Klausner, *op. cit., page 320.*
37. *Ibid.,* page 42.
38. *Midrash Rabbah* on Genesis, chap. 85, sect. 9 (vol. 2, page 795).
39. *Ibid.,* on Numbers, chap. 18, sect. 23 (vol. 2, page 744).
40. *The Midrash on Psalms,* Psalm 90, sect. 12 (vol. 2, page 94).
41. Matthew 22:42-44; Mark 12:35-37; Luke 20:41-44; Epistle to the Hebrews 1:13; chapters 5 to 9.
42. *Universal Jewish Encyclopedia,* vol. 7, page 454, col. 2.
43. In Zechariah 6:13 the Hebrew verb rendered as "He shall be" can be rendered as "there shall be" by a skeptical mind in order to ignore the real import of the prophet's statement. In doing so, the translator would ignore the significance of the word "His" in the expression "His throne" as twice used in that one verse.
44. *The Jewish Encyclopedia,* vol. 12, page 646, col. 1.
45. See BT *Sanhedrin* 38b (page 245) and footnote no. 6.

BIBLIOGRAPHY

HOLY SCRIPTURES

The Holy Scriptures, Jewish Publication Society of America (JPS), Philadelphia, Pa. (1917).

The Twenty-Four Books of the Holy Bible, Hebrew and English, Isaac Leeser's Translation, Hebrew Publishing Co., New York, N.Y. (n.d.).

The Twenty-Four Books of the Holy Scriptures, Alexander Harkavy's Translation, Hebrew Publishing Co., New York, N.Y. (1916).

The Septuagint Version (LXX) in Greek and English, Harper and Bros., New York, N.Y. (n.d.).

TARGUMS

The Targums of Onkelos and Jonathan ben Uzziel on the Pentateuch, J. W. Etheridge's Translation (2 vols.), KTAV Publishing House, Inc., New York, N.Y. (1968).

THE TALMUDS

The Babylonian Talmud (BT), 18 vols., The Soncino Press, London, Eng. (1935-1952).

The Minor Tractates of the Talmud (MTT), 2 vols., The Soncino Press, London, Eng. (1971).

Talmud of Jerusalem (JT), Moses Schwab's Translation, Hermon Press, New York, N.Y. (1969).

MIDRASHIC WORKS

Midrash Rabbah, 10 vols., The Soncino Press, London, Eng. (1961).

The Midrash on Psalms, 2 vols., Wm. G. Braude's Translation, Yale University Press, New Haven, Conn. (1959).

OTHER RABBINICAL WORKS

Pesikta de-Rab Kahana, Wm. G. Braude and Israel J. Kapstein's Translation, Jewish Publication Society of America, Philadelphia, Pa. (1975).

Pesikta Rabbati, 2 vols., W. G. Braude's Translation, Yale University Press, New Haven, Conn. (1968).

Pirke de Rabbi Eliezer, Gerald Friedlander's Translation, Hermon Press, New York, N.Y. (1916).

Philo (Judaeus), 10 vols., F. H. Colson and G. H. Whitaker's Translation, Harvard University Press, Cambridge, Mass. (1971).

Prayer Book for the New Year, A Th. Philips.

ENCYCLOPEDIAS

Encyclopedia Judaica, 16 vols., Macmillan Co., New York (1972).

The Standard Jewish Encyclopedia, W. H. Allen, London, Eng. (1959).

Encyclopaedia Britannica, (11th edition), 29 vols., The Encyclopaedia Britannica Co., New York, N.Y (1910).

The Jewish Encyclopedia, 12 vols., KTAV Publishing House, Inc., New York, N.Y. (1901).

The Universal Jewish Encyclopedia, 10 vols., Universal Jewish Encyclopedia Inc., New York, N.Y. (1939-1943).

MISCELLANEOUS

Cohen, A., *Everyman's Talmud,* E. P. Dutton Co., New York, N.Y.

Cohen, A., *Joshua and Judges,* Soncino Press, London (1959).

Josephus, Flavius, 9 vols., Harvard University Press (HUP), Cambridge, Mass. (1926).

Klausner, Joseph, *Jesus of Nazareth,* Beacon Press, Boston, Mass. (1964).

Klausner, Joseph, *The Messianic Idea in Israel,* The Macmillan Co., New York, N.Y. (1955).

Moore, George Foote , *Judaism in the First Centuries of the Christian Era,* 2 vols., Harvard University Press, Cambridge, Mass. (1962).

Slotki, Judah J., *Daniel, Ezra, Nehemiah,* The Soncino Press, London, Eng. (1966).

White, E. G., *Patriarchs and Prophets,* Pacific Press Publishing Association, Mountain View, Calif. (1958).